MANAGING ME

WHY SOME LEADERS BUILD A REMARKABLE
LEGACY AND OTHERS SADLY CRUMBLE

dr. stephen r. graves

Managing Me: Why Some Leaders Build a
Remarkable Legacy and Others Sadly Crumble
[Revised and Expanded Edition]

Published by KJK Inc. Publishing
P.O. Box 9448
Fayetteville, AR 72702

Details in some anecdotes and stories have been changed to protect the identities of the persons involved.

ISBN 978-1-940794-06-8

Prepared in association with Edit Resource, LLC (editresource.com)

Steve is dedicated to drive conversations, uncover insights, and publish around four themes he is passionate about: Leadership Development, Social Innovation, Practical Faith, and Organizational Strategy.

For more resources from KJK Publishing and to view Steve's blog visit www.stephenrgraves.com

MANAGING ME
WHY SOME LEADERS BUILD A REMARKABLE
LEGACY AND OTHERS SADLY CRUMBLE

"ONE CAN HAVE NO SMALLER
OR GREATER MASTERY THAN
MASTERY OF ONESELF."
—LEONARDO DA VINCI

CHAPTER 1

BEN AND YOU
AND ME

BEN ANDERSON WAS quite a guy, everyone agreed. He was smart, capable, and ambitious. By his early thirties, Ben had taken his dad's hardware store and transformed it into a major construction supplier in the region. He had twenty stores in three states and a staff of nearly two hundred. He was a rising star, a mainstay on the annual East Coast "40 under 40" lists, and he and his wife were a fixture at every major philanthropy event in the community.

In spite of all his success, though, he seemingly hadn't changed. He was still the same down-to-earth, genuine guy he had always been. He never came across as entitled or arrogant. In fact, his authenticity and graciousness seemed almost magnetic. People wanted to be around him, to be a part of what he was doing, to follow him where he was going.

Yet there he sat at the defendant's table in the courtroom, his head in his hands, listening as the judge read the decision: "Guilty on two counts of fraud. Guilty on one count of embezzlement."

Ben's stomach dropped. The room started to spin around him. He sat in disbelief, desperately trying to compose himself.

Suddenly, the sound of the judge's voice snapped him back to attention. "The defendant will return one week from today for sentencing. Do you have any questions?"

"Yes!" Ben wanted to scream. "How can you do this to me? I don't deserve this—I'm a good guy!" But Ben didn't say any of those things. Instead, he simply stood, shook his head, and followed his lawyer out of the courtroom.

As much as some part of him wanted to shout defiantly at the judge and declare his innocence, a greater part of him knew that he deserved everything that was coming. It had been coming for quite some time.

THE ACCOUNTING

A couple of years before the guilty verdict, Ben's company had been in financial straits that no one on the outside would have expected. Ben had taken out several small loans in the company's name to support his own lifestyle and to keep up with the payments on his new home. He expected a huge shipment to one of his leading clients to make up for the deficit, but then he found out that the client had financial problems of its own and was declaring bankruptcy. The order was canceled. So now Ben was in a big hole, and before long the bank would be coming after him and his company, if he didn't do something fast.

Then the idea came to him.

Ben was reviewing an order for another one of his commercial clients. It was for well over a million dollars' worth of goods, and it included thousands of items. He suddenly wondered if anyone would notice if he added a few more units to the order. Almost without thinking, he changed a few quantities from 100 to 120, from 50 to 60, and from 200 to 225. If someone noticed, he figured, he could pass it off as a computer glitch and take the product back.

One week went by, then two, then three. No one noticed.

It turned out that hardly anyone reviewed deliveries from Ben's company when they arrived. They were approved on the front end, and when they arrived on-site, the guys unloading the truck for $8 an hour didn't care. Once the shipping manifest was signed, most customers knew it was too much of a hassle to dispute an order, so they just absorbed the cost and kept going.

Ben tried his ploy again and again. Soon he was changing a dozen orders every day. Just small quantities—$500 here, $1,000 there. It was barely noticeable on million-dollar orders, but by doing it over and over, he was bringing in nearly $150,000 extra every month. Before long, his cash flow problem was gone.

Meanwhile, Ben was expanding into new markets and picking up new clients. He stopped altering orders, and everything was on the up and up again. The previous six months had been brutal, but it looked like things would work out. Sure, the order jiggering may not have been the most honest way to save his company's life, but he had pulled it through. Hundreds of employees and their families were safe because of what he had done. *I did what I had to do*, he told himself.

The weeks went by, the seasons changed, and soon Ben had all but forgotten the fraud he had engaged in. Life was back to normal and things were looking up.

Then one day his phone chirped. "Yes, Mary," Ben said to his assistant in the outer office.

"There are some men here to see you," she replied nervously.

"Who is it?" Ben asked.

"You'd better come out here, Ben."

Ben walked through the door and saw two men in dark suits staring solemnly back at him. He couldn't help but notice their badges prominently displayed for all to see. "Mr. Anderson, we would like to have a word with you."

Ben's stomach tightened and he fought to appear calm. "Of course, come on in."

Over the weeks that followed, Ben learned that one of his clients had noticed a discrepancy in an order, prompting them to review a few more orders. When they realized what was happening, they contacted the local authorities, who then launched a full investigation.

More than two dozen of Ben's clients had been involved and several hundred thousand dollars of fraud had been uncovered.

What happened next was a blur to Ben. Meeting after meeting with lawyers, law enforcement officials, and judges, followed by weeks in court, led to his conviction.

Looking back now, he realized he'd had so many chances to do the right thing, to own his mistakes, to make amends. But he never did. At each turn he justified his actions a little more, pressed down the guilt feelings a little further, and kept going. *How did I get into such bad habits?* he asked himself. *Why wasn't I paying more attention to what I was doing and what the consequences would be? Everybody—including me—thought I was a great guy, so how could I have ruined things for myself, my family, and my company?*

Although he didn't know yet what his sentence would be, he knew he would have a long time to think about these questions in jail. And also, to think about who he would be when he came out the other side of the criminal justice system.

SELF-MANAGEMENT

For most of us, Ben's story is uncomfortably familiar. The details may differ, but we know the basic plot all too well. Success, notoriety, happiness…and then all of a sudden it's gone. We've seen it played out on TV in the lives of politicians, CEOs, and megachurch pastors. It's happened to old friends, business associates, maybe even family members. Each time, we shake our heads in frustration and disbelief and ask, "How could she let that happen?" or "How could he be so stupid?"

From the outside, these stories tend to look like one spectacularly bad decision that collapsed a promising life. In most cases, though, the truth is much less sensational. More

"BEN ASKED HIMSELF, *WHY WASN'T I PAYING MORE ATTENTION TO WHAT I WAS DOING AND WHAT THE CONSEQUENCES WOULD BE?*"

often than not, that "one decision" was just the most glaring in a string of many poor decisions. We arrive to see the burning wreck in the ditch, but we never know about the oil leak, flat tires, and cracked windshield that landed it there.

That's what this book is about. It's about staying out of the ditch. It's about making the right decisions over and over again in the areas that really matter. It isn't about how others affect you. It isn't about how your environment conditions you. Sure, those are variables that impact your outcomes. But the most crucial variable is you. *It is up to you to manage you.* Because for each one of us, that's where everything starts.

I'm not saying that everything is about you or that you are more important than anyone else. I'm certainly not saying that your well-being should be the primary focus of your life. What I am saying is that, if you want to lead well at home, at work, or in your community or church, you had better start by leading yourself well, and you had better keep managing yourself well over time. If you don't—if you get so caught up in managing others that you stop managing your own part of the story—that's when things tend to crumble. That, I think, is the answer to the question "How could he (or she) let that happen?"

This book is about much more than failure in business ethics—Ben Anderson's particular type of downfall. It is about all the ways that men and women can be successful in managing others and yet fail in managing their own lives. They fall short of the productive and flourishing life they wanted for themselves.

This warning about the need for broad and effective self-management should have been taken seriously by …

+ The executive who got promoted into the corner office and then came home to find that the wife he'd been neglecting had moved out
+ The hard worker who kept his head down taking care of business, only to let the opportunity to pursue his real dream pass him by
+ The high achiever who gathered in all the wealth she dreamed of but is now surprised to find how empty she feels inside
+ The tiger in the board room who has plenty of people to respect and fear her but no one who is a friend
+ The workaholic who never gave a thought to caring for his health until he had a heart attack
+ The materialist who directed all his effort toward making a worldly success of himself, only to reach old age and wonder if there might be something to the spiritual perspective after all

You may be like these people, and like Ben, in that you are skilled in managing people and projects. But could you also be failing in the same way they are? In other words, even as you are managing others effectively, are you neglecting to manage yourself? And if that's so, what kinds of risks are you creating? Are other people paying a price? Are you missing out on achieving your full potential? Are you failing to thrive as you'd hoped?

So far, you might not have given a lot of focused attention to managing your own life. You might not have even *thought* about it. If so, it's time for you to tell yourself, "I'm going to manage me!"

SECTION 1

IT'S UP TO ME TO MANAGE ME

CHAPTER 2

THE CORE PRINCIPLE

"WHAT IS THE single most important thing a leader needs to understand or do in order to be successful?"

Throughout the course of my career, I've been asked some version of this question hundreds of times. I've been asked it by Fortune 50 executives, small business owners, nonprofit leaders, and pastors. I've heard the question from naturally charismatic, engaging leaders, and I've heard it from shy, introverted geniuses who lead others out of necessity rather than choice. Almost every time, though, regardless of the person or the situation, the motivation has been the same—leaders want to lead well.

There are, of course, lousy leaders out there who are self-centered and manipulative. But the majority of leaders really want to lead effectively. They aren't necessarily looking for a silver bullet or a magic formula, but they do realize that they can't do everything. They can't read every leadership book, attend every seminar, or listen to every podcast. They need to break through the clutter and get to the essentials. So, when they ask this question, what they're really asking is, "What is the core or foundation of effective leadership? What is the one thing I've got to get right?"

Over the years, I've answered this question a number of ways. I've given specific advice that I knew a particular leader in a particular moment needed to hear. I've shared wisdom learned through my own successes and failures. I've kept it simple and I've made it complex.

I'm glad I shared those varied insights. And yet recently I've wondered if I haven't been getting ahead of myself.

Like most authors, coaches, and speakers working in the leadership space, I tend to focus on what I'll broadly call "leadership skills." If I'm talking with an overly ambitious leader, prone to dreaming and lacking in execution, I may discuss the importance of managing expectations and crafting a realistic and compelling vision. If I'm working with a demanding leader who is inclined to blow up without notice, I'll likely stress the importance of healthy conflict resolution or more effective ways to encourage results. In each case, I'm emphasizing how the leader interacts with and relates to those he or she is leading. I'm emphasizing a leadership skill that can be refined and improved, and the movement is from the leader out.

Ultimately, though, leadership skills are like the walls of a house. They really are important and they really are worth building up, but they are only as strong and as valuable as the foundation upon which they are built. When we start our conversations about leadership at the skill level, we are actually making a pretty significant assumption. We are assuming that the leaders *have* a strong foundation. If they do, the walls of skill can be strong and effective. If they don't—that is, if their foundation is uneven or incomplete—the walls may stand for a while, but eventually they will crack and deteriorate.

What, then, *is* the core or foundation of effective leadership?

By now, you can guess the answer.

It's not managing others well, nor any of the other aspects of leadership. It's about managing oneself, being a leader to oneself.

Pamela Butler said, "There is a person with whom you spend more time than any other, a person who has more influence over you, and more ability to interfere with or to support your growth than anyone else. This ever-present companion is your own self."[1] Each of us, if we want to be successful, must pay attention to this companion and manage ourselves.

"LEADERSHIP SKILLS ARE
LIKE THE WALLS OF A HOUSE.
THEY ARE IMPORTANT AND
WORTH BUILDING UP, BUT
THEY ARE ONLY AS STRONG AS
THE FOUNDATION UPON WHICH
THEY ARE BUILT."

It's surprising how often this principle is overlooked, especially since it has been true as long as there have been leaders. Let me give you a historical example.

THE ORIGINAL COMPANY

In 1540, ten Christian men banded together to form an organization. They had no capital and no business plan and lacked the credentialing we are accustomed to leaders having. But they created a four-hundred-year leadership pipeline that is arguably the most successful and sustainable leadership engine ever created. They embodied the "start with why" premise that Simon Sinek argues in his recent bestseller.[2] They had a vision for honoring God in all they did and even took the name Companions of Jesus to show their dedication to God and His purposes for their lives. Some say that name is the origin of the word *company* we use so broadly today.

From ten friends in Rome, the Companions of Jesus—or the Jesuits, as they became known—scattered all over the world to become successful educators, linguists, theologians, diplomats, astronomers, and other professionals. Today there are more than seven hundred Jesuit schools worldwide (Georgetown, St. Bonaventure, and Gonzaga among them) still following the organization's original architecture of building remarkable leadership.

The Jesuits' leadership model was anchored in four basic tenets: self-awareness, ingenuity, love and service to others, and heroism. Those in the organization were expected to pay attention to and develop these qualities in themselves if they were hoping to influence others. So the model was about a leader managing himself effectively and then from that foundation applying his unique skill set to make a contribution.

"YOU AND I MUST
EFFECTIVELY MANAGE OUR
OWN LIFE BEFORE WE EARN
THE MORAL AUTHORITY
TO STEP INTO MANAGING
SOMEONE ELSE'S LIFE."

This model works in so many arenas, not just religious organizations. Still today it's true that, in order to lead others well, you must first lead yourself well. You must effectively manage the areas of your life that matter before you can manage any area of someone else's life.

Most leaders want to be effective in the short term and the long term. Most also desire fulfillment and a respectable legacy. Leaders in all kinds of for-profit and not-for-profit organizations, in fact, become more effective in their work, as well as more satisfied and content with their lives, when they pay attention to what they're spending time on and how they're making choices.

I can think of many people who exemplify, to me, the payoff that comes from great self-management. One is named Robert.

PRODUCTIVE IN EVERY STAGE OF LEADERSHIP

I have been going to the same church for almost thirty years. Actually, my wife and I do more than just attend—we are actively engaged, just as we have been since we joined the church. Let me tell you a bit about the church, and then I want to tell you about Robert.

The church was launched in the fall of 1983 with seven families and a young, energetic leader named Robert who agreed to help get it off the ground and serve as the directional leader. Like many churches in high-growth areas in the United States, our church has steadily grown, year over year, expanding its depth, breadth, and reach. It would easily be classified as one of the largest and most impactful churches in our state and maybe even the country. But we have never kept those kinds of measurements, so I am not certain where we stack up. The church has unquestionably shaped our community and positively impacted tens of thousands of folks around the globe, and Robert has directed that scaling.

I have watched my friend and pastor, Robert, serve the church as our directional leader for thirty years. I have also watched Robert tend to his own soul and self-management every year of those thirty years. Effectiveness, sustainability, and fulfillment have stamped Robert's leadership, giving him a remarkable legacy. Is he a perfect leader? No, of course not. Nor is he the only pastor on our church's staff managing his or her own life well. But I've had a front-row seat to his leadership for thirty years, and I can tell that self-leadership has been a personal priority for him. And I've been taking notes.

At our church, we recently transitioned to the next generation of leadership, and Robert has taken a new seat on the bus. Why do I bring this up? Because often a transition exposes a founding leader's lack of growth and personal maturity. For example, years ago I worked with a national leader who aborted three succession plans because of his inability to deal with all the realities that accompanied giving up his lead role. That sad scenario gets played out, with variations, all the time. But not with Robert.

I remember telling my wife thirty years ago that I felt our church would be a place of growth, challenge, and health—and it has been. It still is. I firmly believe this is in large part due to Robert's commitment to self-management and self-leadership.

Over the pages that follow, we'll explore why self-management is so important. I'll address some of the most persistent issues we face as we manage ourselves, and I'll conclude with some practical guidance to help you manage yourself better.

CHAPTER 3

IS SELF-MANAGEMENT
REALLY THAT IMPORTANT?

I AM PROPOSING that the effectiveness of a leader does not first depend on innate ability or the mastery of skills but is instead determined primarily by the effectiveness with which the leader manages him- or herself. In fact, I would go so far as to claim that this issue of self-management is the foundation upon which a leader's effectiveness is built. As self-management goes, so goes the leader.

As you read these words, you may question the volume of emphasis I'm placing on self-management. You might be thinking, *I agree that it is important, but what makes it so important that I should consider it the foundation of leadership?* This is a reasonable question and one that I think it is worth our time to consider.

Recently, while reading the *Harvard Business Review*, I ran across a thought about leaders and their focus. It caught my attention because almost every leader I know is working on having better focus. In the article, Daniel Goleman said, "The key to focus is not filtering out distractions but seeing what matters."[3] That perspective immediately resonated with me. It is surely true.

But identifying what matters and what doesn't matter isn't always easy. I wish there were some High Matter Rating Alarm that would go off when we put the wrong weight on something—you begin investing time and attention and resources in something of low matter rating, and the lights and alarm starts screaming. But there isn't. We have to make judgment calls, decision by decision, day by day, about where to put our focus.

Self-management is deserving of the highest matter rating we can give anything. Without effective self-management, none of the other stuff matters as much. Without it, you can't lead well, and you certainly can't lead well over time. It's a non-negotiable. Here are some reasons why.

AUTHENTICITY

Individuals want to be led well. They want leaders with vision and purpose who live compelling lives. No one lines up to follow the guy whose business is in a shambles and whose personal life is constantly in crisis. We want leaders who model their message, who are buying what they're selling. This is why spiritual leaders with a strong personal testimony are so impactful. It's why people want to listen to Warren Buffett's advice about finance, and why overweight personal trainers don't have many clients. We want leaders who have not only done what they're asking us to do but are still doing it. Albert Schweitzer said, "Example is not the main thing in influencing others. It is the only thing."[4]

If it's at church, we want pastors with a vibrant personal faith. If it's in the office, we want leaders who make wise strategic decisions, are good stewards of company resources, and seem to have some degree of self-control. At home, we follow when a leader loves and serves others well. In short, we want to follow authentic leaders. We don't want to follow leaders who just appear successful; we want leaders who *are* authentically successful, who are really living out their message, not just pretending to when the cameras are rolling.

I finally met Michael a couple of years ago. I had heard about him and his company for over a decade. Back when my business partner and I were publishing the *Life@Work Journal*, I first ran into Michael's legendary reputation. Often we hear amazing things about someone, and then when we finally meet him or her, we are left disappointed (or even feel duped, if we

"THE KEY TO FOCUS IS
NOT FILTERING OUT
DISTRACTIONS BUT SEEING
WHAT MATTERS."

are fully honest). Mike, though, was all he had been advertised to be…and even more.

I recently received a text from another friend who had just met Michael and said about him, "Man, what an authentic and meaningful guy."

I shot back a text saying, "Wait till you see the stuff beneath the skin and surface."

Michael built his company around an aggressive set of values that deliver both personal dignity for his employees and a global commitment to the common good. And he has stayed the course for decades. His company perpetually competes worldwide to be in the top five of its class. With that kind of public exposure, there is no hiding with authenticity. Either you are or you are not.

Even though *authenticity* has become an overused buzzword for everything from food to clothes, don't discount the importance of what it stands for. People can spot phoniness a mile away. They'll know when you're just putting on a show, when your life doesn't match the image you're projecting. You may think that the particulars of your life have nothing to do with your ability to lead, but others will call it what it is— hypocrisy—and they won't tolerate it.

This lack of patience for inauthentic leaders is especially pronounced with the Millennial generation. If you want to lead them in business, in ministry, or at home, you had better make authenticity a priority.

I recently had a meal with a round table of men and women all in the early season of their work and representing a smattering of vocations. We were talking about their ambitions, their respective companies, and the leadership they were under during this season. It was eye opening to again hear firsthand the dramatic difference in what a Millennial values in a leader, compared to what older folks value in a leader. The Millennials who worked for a boss or company full of duplicity wanted to get out as fast as they could. Absent authenticity, pay and perks just don't hold an employee like they did a generation ago.

But simply letting others down isn't the only conflict tied to inauthenticity. Hypocrisy creates an inner dissonance that disturbs our rest and peace. An inauthentic person is always off balance.

What does all this have to do with self-management?

To be a leader worth following, to live an authentically compelling life, you've got to be trying to manage yourself well. That kind of life doesn't happen by accident. It requires intentionality and focus.

UNHEALTHY LEADERS MAKE UNHEALTHY FOLLOWERS

I have said that individuals want to be led by someone worth following. The reverse is just as true: leaders want to lead people worth leading. No leader wants to be the captain of a team that can't shoot straight. When leaders are forced to spend all of their time and energy micromanaging, demanding, and dragging their followers along, they quickly lose the desire to lead. What leaders in this situation often fail to realize, though, is this simple truth: healthy leaders make healthy followers, and unhealthy leaders make unhealthy followers.

If a business executive is loose with company resources, if he always flies first class and charges everything on his corporate card, he shouldn't be surprised when his subordinates tend to be liberal with their own discretionary budgets.

If a pastor works around the clock, regularly neglecting his family in favor of work, he may notice crumbling marriages among his staff and lay leaders.

Years ago I worked with the CEO of a large company, and one of the things we were trying to do was upgrade his senior leadership team to get ready for a transition. One leader was clearly at the bottom of the scoreboard with regard to morality, ethics, and commitment to growing the enterprise value of the company. To me, it was obvious. What I wasn't ready for was the personal and corporate irresponsibility that poured straight downhill from that senior leader to his thousands of employees. When we looked deep into that particular vertical, we saw Dumpster fire after Dumpster fire. The senior leader's lack of self-control and honesty were magnified times two down in his business unit.

Samuel Rima, in *Leading from the Inside Out*, states: "The way in which a leader conducts his personal life does, in fact, have a profound impact on his ability to exercise effective public leadership. There is a direct correlation between self-leadership and public leadership."[5] The manner in which you, as a leader, approach everything from finances to relationships to ethics directly impacts how those you are leading will approach those issues. If you want to lead a team, organization, or ministry worth leading, it is absolutely necessary that you first ensure that you are taking care of what matters in your life, and you do so in a way that you're comfortable with others emulating. Again, this won't happen by accident. It only happens with effective self-management.

SUCCESS THAT LASTS

We've all encountered a successful business leader whose personal life and finances are a mess. We've listened to sermons

"EXAMPLE IS NOT
THE MAIN THING IN
INFLUENCING OTHERS. IT
IS THE ONLY THING."
– ALBERT SCHWEITZER

from pastors who we knew had questionable ethical standards but also had rapidly growing churches. It seems, then, at least at first glance, that I've overstated my case. It seems that it is, in fact, possible to be a successful leader and at the same time, to be a lousy self-manager.

Before you put down this book and write me off, let me issue a few words of caution and clarification.

While it may very well be possible to manage your own life and work poorly and still be a successful leader *for a while*, in my thirty-plus years of coaching, business, and ministry, I've yet to encounter an ineffective self-manager who had real success over the long term. Sure, like you, I've seen and even worked with people who seem to be the exception, who appear to be able to lead well regardless of their own health. But I've also seen that over time these exceptions *always* run smack into reality. Some become a national headline story of disaster and deception. Some just erode a piece of community goodwill. Some inject poison or place a question mark on their family tree. But regardless, a lack of care for yourself will catch up with you at some point—and probably catch up with some of those around you too. Even though a corrupt leader may appear to be flourishing, he or she is really teetering on the edge of moral or literal bankruptcy, and eventually the accounting catches up.

Almost without exception, when leaders experience the type of failure that removes them from leadership, poor *self-management* is a significant factor. I'm not talking about a failed business strategy that gets you fired. I'm talking about moral, ethical, and relational collapses that negate both your ability to lead and the willingness of others to follow you. That's what happened to Ben Anderson (Chapter 1). It's happened to many others as well.

To lead well over time, to make a lasting impact in your business, ministry, or family, you simply have to be managing yourself well. Not perfectly, but well. Otherwise, you may experience sudden spurts of spectacular success that wither when time, pressure, and scrutiny are applied.

I hope I've already got you convinced. I hope you're ready to make self-management the top priority it needs to be if you want to be an effective leader who is satisfied with your own life and legacy. If so, it's time to seize the message for yourself.

CHAPTER 4

IT'S UP TO YOU...
SO OWN IT!

MY HOUSE IS quieter than ever. My three children are all grown and out of the house, making my wife and me officially empty nesters. As we continue to adjust to this new stage of life, we find ourselves still talking about the kids over dinner and bike rides. As we do so, two memory tracks play out.

One track is all about the fun, the laughter, and the specific stories attached to each of our kids. From first steps to first games to graduations, proud moments spring to mind and we look back with grateful hearts.

The other memory track begins to play at certain moments, such as when we run into young friends who have just had a baby, or when I talk to a client who recently adopted a child, or when my wife and I speak with an exhausted and frustrated mom of a toddler at church. Then an entirely different type of memory comes rushing back. Suddenly, as if it had happened yesterday, I remember sleepless nights and hours of crying. I remember arguments over bed and vegetables. I remember baby-proofing and constant redirecting from light sockets, fireplaces, and sharp edges. I remember exasperated pronouncements of "That's not fair!" Perhaps more than anything else, I remember (with a shudder) the helpless and frustrated feeling of trying to do what's best for someone who has no regard for his or her own well-being. After all, isn't that what your first couple years of parenting are—trying to keep an irrational little maniac alive, stopping him or her from diving out of the crib, drinking cleaning supplies, and running into the street?

While you will always care deeply about the welfare of your children, in those first years you care about it much more than they themselves do. Even though they don't know it, most children have a small army of family, teachers, and physicians looking out for their best interest. They have to, or they wouldn't survive!

Here's my point: When we become an adult, that army becomes a contingent of one. When we're grown up, there is no team assigned to look out for us. We have to look out for ourselves. I am not downplaying the legitimate role of community, but community doesn't manage our lives as adults.

It's up to you to identify priorities and make the right decisions for yourself. No amount of nagging family, encouraging friends, or concerned co-workers is going to make you eat healthy, or go to the gym, or read a book instead of watching TV. When it comes to self-management, when it comes to making good decisions in the areas of your adult life that matter most, the responsibility is entirely yours. That is a sobering reality of growing up.

Sure, your family will care, your organization will care, your church group will care, but the management of your life will never be a priority for anyone in the way it should be for you. It's up to you, and you've got to own it. You can't outsource it. You can't delegate it. You can't build a process or system, hit "start," and walk away. There is no way to automate self-management, and it won't happen on accident. (Nothing that matters does.) You've got to make self-management a priority, and you've got to keep it as a priority.

The alternative is to wait for a crisis to force you to make self-management a priority. Unfortunately, this is how many of us approach the issue. We wait until the final notice comes from the bank to start getting our finances in order. We wait until we're lying in the hospital bed to start taking care of our health. We wait until our spouse has left and our kids won't talk to us to start making relationships a priority. When we have no other choice, we act. The crisis forces us into a period

"THE MOST EFFECTIVE SELF-MANAGEMENT IS CONSISTENT. IT ISN'T MARKED BY GRAND ONE-TIME GESTURES AND SWEEPING CHANGES BUT RATHER BY REGULAR REFLECTION AND CONSISTENT ACTION."

of clarity, and we react with urgency. Change occasioned by crisis, however, rarely lasts. When things get better and stresses subside, we slip into our old routines and wait for the next disaster to shake us into wakefulness.

Eventually, though, the damage from the wake-up call may prove too great to repair. Even though we can always make changes and can always take positive steps, we cannot always undo the consequences that have already come. This is why the most effective self-management is consistent. It isn't marked by grand one-time gestures and sweeping changes but rather by regular reflection and consistent action. It takes constant attention, it takes constant focus, and it requires day-in and day-out choices at a level only you can provide.

So don't wait. Don't look around for help. Look inward and take ownership of your own life and lifestyle.

As you do, here are a few principles that I've found helpful along the way.

YOUR CONTEXT MATTERS, BUT...

In the second half of this book, I'll discuss six choices that I believe represent the critical building blocks of a well-managed, healthy life. They don't add up to a magic formula, and they don't make up the totality of what it means to be an effective self-manager, but they are a starting point, a place from which to grow.

As you read through these choices, you'll likely notice that they aren't accompanied by a step-by-step implementation plan. I don't tell you exactly what a choice will look like in your life or even how to make it. I don't do this because it is not possible and, if it were, it wouldn't be particularly helpful. Self-management is a context-specific discipline. It depends greatly on your personal wiring and your unique situation.

What it means for you to make a certain decision will likely look very different from what it means for me to make that same decision. So, for example, while I can tell you that an effectively managed life successfully juggles the multiple opportunities and assignments of your personal and professional worlds, I can't tell you what those assignments and opportunities will be nor which ones to take and which ones to reject. It is up to you to take the principles discussed and apply them to your life and work. Your context matters, and so you should take stock of it and let it inform your decisions about what effective self-management looks like for you.

The danger is that, rather than letting our context shape the contours of our self-management, we allow it to become an excuse for poor self-management. We say, "I would be better at nurturing relationships if this or that had not happened to me" or "I would more effectively manage my finances if only I had the opportunities that So-and-so had."

If we aren't careful, we can easily rationalize away our own responsibility to manage ourselves. We can make the entire process about what others have done to us, rather than about what we can do ourselves.

My mother warned me about this danger when I was a young man. Even though my father had left and our lives were difficult, my mother often reminded me that I still had a choice. Either I could play the victim and go through life blaming my dad or I could take responsibility for myself, for the decisions I made, and for the life I lived.

What my mother was trying to communicate is a hard truth about self-management. Even though in one sense your context matters a lot, in another it doesn't matter at all. Regardless of what has happened to you or where you find yourself, self-management is still a non-negotiable and it is still your responsibility.

NOT JUST *AN ISSUE OF WILLPOWER*

At several points already in this book, I've referred to self-management as a discipline, and in many ways that is exactly what it is. Like any skill, it takes conscious effort and attention to develop and refine. It requires that you make certain decisions while rejecting others, and it is, at least in some sense, a matter of will. I can help you define the parameters of a well-managed life. I can line you up and point you in the right direction. But ultimately it's up to you to actually choose to take the steps to make it happen.

This is an important principle of self-management. Without this type of personal commitment and sense of responsibility, effective self-management simply can't happen. At the same time, though, it's perhaps equally important that we realize that we can't do it totally alone, that we cannot achieve effective self-management solely through willpower and sheer determination. You can't white-knuckle your way to a well-managed life; it's simply too big and too difficult a task for that.

To try and manage every part of your life, and to try and do it through self-will alone, would be the equivalent of a person who has never run a mile announcing that he will race in a marathon and that he doesn't need any help preparing. More likely than not, he'll abandon his goal by the second week. But if instead the novice runner sets his goal and then hires a trainer to develop his plan, visits a nutritionist to design his meals, and joins a running group to train alongside, he has dramatically increased his chances of success. Yes, the decisions to run each day and eat right are still up to him, but

---

"SELF-MANAGEMENT IS
A CONTEXT-SPECIFIC
DISCIPLINE. IT DEPENDS
GREATLY ON YOUR PERSONAL
WIRING AND YOUR UNIQUE
SITUATION."

---

now he has surrounded himself with resources, tools, and accountability to help him along the way.

In order to be effective self-managers, we need the same things in our lives. We need to make use of every tool and resource at our disposal. We need to read books, have conversations, and listen to advice. We need to build sustainable processes and surround ourselves with friends who will hold us accountable and challenge us to do better.

I have a friend, Lane, who travels all the time. When he checks into his hotel, he always asks them to turn his movie options off right then. Lane says it is a simple action that helps him fend off the temptation to waste time or view things he has already determined are not good for his soul.

We need a plan and the resources to execute it. Without these things, likely all we're left with are good intentions. Like the naive marathoner, we've set a worthy goal but have little hope of achieving it.

IT'S NOT ALL ABOUT YOU

By the very nature of the term, *self-management* implies a certain inward focus. It's inherently about you—about your priorities, your decisions, your life—and it's ultimately your responsibility. While this is all certainly true and definitely worth remembering, we must also remember the outward aspect of self-management, what I call the "so that" and the "others first" mentality.

We should want to be effective self-managers *so that* we can be successful leaders at home, at the office, and in our churches. We want to manage ourselves well in order to put *others first* and be leaders worth following. Yes, it is about my reputation and influence. But it is also about those around me who have given me their trust. It is hard to become a narcissist obsessed with yourself when you build a habit of making others equally important.

In other words, effective self-management should never become an end in itself. When it does, when all our efforts and work end with us, we're left with a shallow version of self-help that nobody wants to follow.

You might be saying, "I get that, but isn't there a balance? Doesn't good self-management benefit both us and others?"

Good question. And here's how I would present my answer.

Some people moved into adulthood thinking they were the center of every narrative. Every conversation, every encounter, every spotlight was for them and them alone. So those with quick-trigger tendencies to be focused on themselves should learn to make others a priority.

Meanwhile, others moved into adulthood wired to make everyone around them happy at any cost. These folks with hyper-people-pleasing tendencies should turn back toward an internal set of values they operate by.

So yes, there *is* a balance, and getting the right balance depends on where you start.

When I manage me, I am creating a leader worth following. But I am also creating a leader who can enjoy a deeper, more abiding sense of inner peace and contentment. Managing me yields both external and internal fruit that compounds and builds on itself.

Now, I know you want to get started on the practical stuff—the specifics of self-management. That's coming up next. You'll see that there are some key areas where you can begin making changes to run your own life better so that you are leading others better and experiencing a personal payoff.

SECTION 2

SIX CHOICES FOR A NO-REGRETS LIFE

CHAPTER 5

A LIFE WITHOUT REGRETS

I ONCE HEARD the late Joe Aldrich, a university president, say, "When you get to the end of your life and there are nothing but memories to look back on, are you going to be full of regret and remorse—or the opposite?"

How would you answer that? If you knew the end of your life were coming next month, how would you feel about the ways you've spent your time and what you've accomplished up to this point? Would you be more regretful or more thankful?

My intention is not to make you feel bad or place guilt on you. It's certainly not to make you want to give up. In fact, my goal is the opposite! I want to motivate you to make some specific changes in your self-management to set yourself up for success and satisfaction. I've seen time and again that better self-management can turn a life around.

Whatever your history is, if you make changes now, you can build a future that will enable you to look back, not with regrets and remorse but with gratitude and deep contentment. You will experience a life of passion and vitality. It will be a life without major regrets.

Now, when I dare to say that you can have a no-regrets life, I'm not claiming that you can erase the mistakes of the past or escape all their consequences. Nor am I suggesting that from here on out you won't ever stub your toe, have a bad Monday, or run out of gas. But you *can* manage things in your life so that, when you look back, you'll be able to see that you did well in the important areas of life.

You notice that I am not talking narrowly about success in your job as a leader. I'm talking about your *whole* life. Let's define success broadly.

YOUR LIFE'S COMPOSITE SCORECARD

Imagine that you ask your child how his latest report card looks.

He says, "Great! Well, there is one F on there. But that's okay, because there are also a couple of A's."

Would you agree that the report card was great? If it were me, I would say, "Son, I'm glad to hear about those A's. But wait a minute! What about that F in math? An F is unacceptable. That kind of performance throws off your grade point average, and frankly it creates some doubt about your future schooling success."

Similarly, I like to tell the leaders I coach that they have a composite scorecard for their life. It's like a student's report card in that it rates performance in a number of different areas (only they know exactly which areas matter most to them). Doing well in one or two areas is not good enough if they're failing in another. They need to become more balanced in their striving. Although they are hardworking, they need to be hardworking in a way that creates vitality across the whole spectrum of what matters to them.

I don't know if this describes the kind of situation you find yourself in, but I can say this: If your scorecard isn't looking good in every category, then you can change it. You're already a leader—so you have the skills to improve. You know your subject: you. You have the access and the freedom to make changes in your own life. You just need to know what to do.

Let me put this in terms that will help you compare leadership and self-leadership.

"WHEN YOU GET TO THE
END OF YOUR LIFE AND
THERE ARE NOTHING
BUT MEMORIES TO LOOK
BACK ON, ARE YOU GOING
TO BE FULL OF REGRET
AND REMORSE—OR THE
OPPOSITE?" – JOE ALDRICH

SYNCHRONIZED SCALING

Generally speaking, everyone wants to scale his or her business, ministry, organization, or idea. It is what we talk about, scheme toward, and design our strategy against. And generally speaking, unless you have a strategic reason not to scale up (such as a forced pause to let the market, your culture, or resources catch up), scaling is a good idea. But did you know that most effective leaders practice some version of what I call *synchronized scaling?*

Mentally, most of us attach the term *synchronized* to the water sports of the Olympics or the SNL spoof of synchronized swimming. Have you ever watched synchronized divers? Two people are harnessed together, not literally, but in every other way. They look alike in size and uniform. They perform as one unit coming off the board, twisting and entering the water at the exact same second with the exact same form. But the big deal is that they are scored together. There is no independent rating; they only get one score, and it is given for how they performed as a unit.

Similarly, there are two sides to leadership scaling that you must synchronize and treat as a unit: leading yourself and leading your organization. Yes, they are two separate interests, but they are inextricably connected and must be treated as one scorecard. To score in one but fail in the other will not bring the ultimate fulfillment, effectiveness, and legacy you desire.

Remember my friend Ben at the opening of the book? He abandoned managing himself, focusing only on one side of leadership, and he paid dearly. Sometimes leaders lead everything and manage everyone but themselves.

Remember my pastor, Robert? In contrast to Ben, he practiced synchronized scaling, leading himself and leading his organization's growth at the same time. As he's transitioning out of church leadership, his legacy is strong and he has deep fulfillment in his heart for what he's been a part of.

I want to show you how to be more like Robert and less like Ben in synchronized scaling.

THE GAUGES OF LIFE

Throughout my years of advising executives, business owners, and entrepreneurs of all stripes, I've identified six key choices to bring about changes before negative consequences become irreversible. Together, they can channel your passion to help you thrive and flourish and experience broad fulfillment in your life.

I think of these choices as "the gauges of life." Let me tell you what I mean.

I once owned a consulting firm that grew so fast we needed to buy an airplane and hire a couple of full-time pilots. For one thing, we wanted our team to have quality family lives, and so we made it possible for them to come home quickly from distant meeting places. Over the years, we practically flew the wings off that small private plane.

One day I was flying in the plane and was sitting up front, where I began asking the pilot about the gauges. "These are the critical ones," he said in his explanation, pointing to three or four gauges on the dashboard. "The others are important too. But if you want to get home tonight for dinner with your family, these are the ones you keep your eyes on all the time."

There are probably a lot of different things you could do to help manage your own life and reach your full created potential. But like the critical gauges of an airplane, the six choices I'm going describe are actions you simply cannot overlook if you want to achieve your goals in life. Learn these valuable action steps. Practice them. Make them a part of your standard operating procedure. They'll keep you on course to your desired destination.

A Spanish proverb tells us, "What the fool does in the end, the wise man does in the beginning." With these six gauges, you can become wise.

"WHAT THE FOOL DOES IN
THE END, THE WISE MAN
DOES IN THE BEGINNING."

CHAPTER 6

CHOICE 1: WILL YOU ESTABLISH STRATEGIC CLARITY?

A PROFESSOR IN his lecture auditorium set an empty glass jar on the table in front of him, and then he placed several rocks in it until they reached the top of the jar. He asked the watching students, "Is the jar full?"

The students said it was.

Next, the professor added pebbles to the jar, shaking it so that the pebbles settled around the rocks. Again he asked if the jar was full. And again the students agreed that it was.

Then the professor poured in sand until it filled all the remaining spaces in the jar.

"This jar is like your life," the professor said. "Notice that I put the rocks in first. They represent the big stuff that matters in your life—your relationships, your dreams, whatever's most important to you. They're not everything in life. There's surprising room for small stuff too, as we found out. But make sure you put the big stuff, the rocks, into your life first, because everything else is just pebbles and sand."

In life, we have to stay focused on the things that matter most. For most leaders, clarity starts with establishing which of many possible priorities take precedence. As Stephen Covey said, "The main thing is to keep the main thing the main thing."[6]

But how do we determine what the "main thing" is?

PRINCIPLES FOR PRIORITIZING

Spotting the things that matter most is not always easy. Truth be told, on any given week we have all kinds of things competing for our time and attention. And the difficulty is life doesn't always self-select. During times of crisis, emergency, or epiphany, the most important things float to the top. But the rest of the time we have to sort, weigh, and select.

Here are a few things to keep in mind:

+ *Not everything carries the same weight.* In life, some things are simply more important than others. It's like the tests you took in school. Some questions were worth twenty points, some worth ten, and some worth only two. If you spent the same amount of time on each question, it probably didn't turn out well. Likewise, we have to fight the tendency to spend too much time on the two-point issues in life. As one writer said, "Things which matter most must never be at the mercy of things which matter least."[7]

+ *You have limited capacity.* Regardless of how smart or talented you may be, you can't effectively manage everything.

  Think of your personal capacity as a tabletop. It has only so much space. Sure, you can stack stuff to fit more on the tabletop, but eventually you're going to run out of room. When you try to press these limits, at least one area will suffer. Something will fall off your tabletop. Working harder and harder to fit things onto your tabletop, instead of recognizing that you have limited capacity, becomes counterproductive. As Peter Drucker said, "There is nothing so useless as doing efficiently that which should not be done at all."[8]

+ *Priorities are not set in stone.* While some priorities will remain high-level priorities (such as maintaining your health and your spiritual wellness) for your entire life, many others—perhaps school, hobbies, and work—will be more or less important, and demand more or less attention, during certain seasons. To manage yourself effectively over time, you must learn to identify these changes in season and adjust your focus accordingly.

"CLARITY STARTS WITH
ESTABLISHING WHICH
OF MANY POSSIBLE
PRIORITIES TAKE
PRECEDENCE."

WHAT HAPPENS WITHOUT STRATEGIC CLARITY?

When Jim Collins released his famous book *Good to Great* in 2001, he listed Circuit City as one of his "great" organizations. As we now know, not long after the book was released, Circuit City fell from greatness, went into decline, and eventually filed for bankruptcy. Speaking about the company's demise, former CEO Alan Wurtzel noted that the company's leadership had done a lot of things right. They tracked sales and plotted growth. But they missed something much more significant: caring for people. To put it another way, they lost track of what mattered most. They spent time on plenty of worthwhile things but neglected what was truly significant.[9]

Just like Circuit City, if we, as individuals, don't establish a clear sense of priorities, or a plan for maintaining those priorities, our tendency will always be to address the loudest and most urgent issue...even if it isn't the most important. The squeaky wheel really does get the grease. The only problem is, the squeaky wheel might not be the wheel that most needs our attention.

Have you ever considered just how many things are clamoring for your attention? Spouse, children, children's activities, extended family, health, bills, church, work, friends, social obligations, hobbies. I bet you could add to the list.

But did you notice that none of those items were bad things? In fact, they were all good things that we should pay attention to.

This is where strategic clarity comes in. Strategic clarity helps us sort the merely worthwhile from the truly significant. It helps us remember that the urgent and the significant are not always the same thing, that the loud and shiny things aren't always the strategic and noteworthy things.

WHAT KEEPS US FROM STRATEGIC CLARITY?

If strategic clarity is so important, why don't we do a better job of establishing it in our own lives? There are many reasons. For starters:

+ We're blinded by stubbornness, ignorance, arrogance, or a self-centered agenda.
+ We're overwhelmed by the volume of life's demands.
+ We're too easily distracted by things that don't really— Hey, look at that bird!
+ We're too rigid and tactical.

Do any of those mistakes make you wince because they sound familiar? And if so, do any corrections come to mind?

And then there's the bigger question: In your life right now, what ought to be high priority and what ought to be low priority? Don't get caught up with the lower-priority issues at the expense of the highest-priority one.

Maybe the overlooked top priority for you is an issue at work. For example, maybe you know that your company needs to innovate new product lines if it's going to continue to be an industry leader, but you're letting your focus stay stuck on your legacy business.

Or maybe it's something more personal. It could be that you've been so focused on work that you've stopped working out at the gym and watching what you eat, even though your doctor says your health condition could take you out of the game entirely if you're not careful. Or maybe your spouse or your kids are looking to you to show them by your actions that you value them most.

You don't want to look back on this time later in your life and think, *Yeah, I was keeping busy, but I wasn't busy with what I should have been busy with.* You'll want to think, *Whatever else I may have let slide along the way, I took care of what really mattered.* Getting your priorities right is a big part of managing yourself for the future you want.

Figure out what's most important to accomplish in your life right now. Then do that. And remember, as Andy Stanley says, "We don't drift in good directions. We discipline and prioritize ourselves there."[10]

"STRATEGIC CLARITY
HELPS US SORT THE
MERELY WORTHWHILE
FROM THE TRULY
SIGNIFICANT."

1. Have I lost my footing with regard to the priorities of life? Am I simply going through the motions?
2. Is there an issue or past experience that has handcuffed, bushwhacked, or paralyzed my passion and clarity for life?
3. Do the speed, complexity, and myriad options of life feel like a furious European roundabout, spinning me in a circle and creating confusion, frustration, and fear?
4. Am I using creative thinking, analytical thinking, big-picture thinking, and bottom-line thinking to sort and tackle the critical matters of life?
5. Am I anchored to a promising future and a compelling vision?
6. Do I see and sense the mission-critical elements of life?

1. *Think* before you *do*. Always.
2. Install a system I call 5/20/60/300. Dedicate five minutes a day, twenty minutes a week, sixty minutes a month, and three hundred minutes (a half day) per year to focused reflection on sorting the noise from the priorities. At least once a day, take five minutes and ask yourself what things you must get done tomorrow and during the rest of the week. Jot those things down and use them as a mental map to guide you. And then at least once a week take twenty minutes to reflect more deeply. And then layer on a monthly review as well as an annual review.
3. Don't be scared to slow down and analyze all the things screaming for your attention. Draft a short list, assign scores, and make yourself prioritize your activities. As a Japanese proverb says, "Vision without action is a daydream, but action without vision is a nightmare."

CHAPTER 7

CHOICE 2: WILL YOU MAKE YOUR CONTRIBUTION TO THE WORLD?

A WALL STREET investment banker found himself growing weary of his work, and his meteoric success put him in a position to do something about it. Even though he was only in his thirties, he told me he wanted to quit work and retire. In my role as his executive coach, I advised him to take time off and craft a vision for where he might flex his commercial muscles during the next season of his life.

"I will never work again," he said.

I was unconvinced. I bet him that he'd be back at work within eighteen months. And it wasn't long before I collected on that bet—all $20.

How did I know? Because I understood a fundamental truth that my young friend had not yet grasped—we are hardwired to work. We are built to make a contribution to society until the day we die, and the work we do is not merely a biological obligation but is an essential part of a balanced, healthy life. As Fyodor Dostoevsky said, "Deprived of meaningful work, men and women lose their reason for existence: they go stark, raving mad."[11] That is why I won my $20 bet with my friend from NYC.

A BROKEN VIEW

Unfortunately, this isn't how many of us think about work, is it? For most of us, our motivation to work pretty much boils down to two things. First, we work because we have to. Our bills aren't going to pay themselves; no one is giving us the money; and we haven't had any luck playing scratch-off lottery, so...we work. Second, we work so that one day we won't have to work. We work not only to pay this month's rent but also so that someday we can finally stop working! We've probably got a magic number or age in mind, when we'll finally get to kick back on the beach or the golf course and just take it easy.

In short, we see work as a necessary evil. It's an unavoidable and unfortunate part of life that keeps us from doing what we really want to be doing. If we won the lottery tomorrow, we'd be done. We'd send a text to Human Resources from our new boat and never look back.

What if, as I suggested above, this view is broken? What if thinking about work like this—as something we can't wait to be rid of—is a big part of the reason work is so hard? What if it's a mistake to try to shed our work?

Stephen Covey said, "You can retire from a job, but don't ever retire from making extremely meaningful contributions in life."[12] What if he's right?

REDEEMING WORK

The apostle Paul touched on this subject when he told his friends in the city of Thessalonica, "Make it your ambition to lead a quiet life, to mind your own business and work with your hands, just as we told you."[13]

That first phrase—"Make it your ambition to lead a quiet life"—isn't suggesting that we move into a monastery or ditch our iPhones. A possible paraphrase is this: "Strive to have no *turmoil* or *noise*. Be at calm within yourself."

The later phrase "Work with your hands" is self-explanatory. Work hard. Get to the end of your day and lie in bed satisfied that you have expended effort on something worth the effort.

You'll notice that Paul doesn't list which jobs we should consider and which we should avoid. He goes beyond things that usually concern us, like industry and job title, to get to the heart of the matter. He says *this* is what work should look like, regardless of the task.

"DEPRIVED OF MEANINGFUL WORK, MEN AND WOMEN LOSE THEIR REASON FOR EXISTENCE: THEY GO STARK, RAVING MAD."
– FYODOR DOSTOEVSKY

Following on the path that Paul points us toward, I believe there are some fundamental characteristics that all work should share.

- *Work should be meaningful.* The work we do should matter. It should have meaning and importance.

  Interestingly, finding meaning in your work has a lot more to do with you than with your job. One of the most significant problems we have in how we think about work is that we tend to think certain jobs matter more than others. We think that what we are doing might not be bad, but those folks working at charities or volunteering at the local shelter—they are doing really important work.

  Of course, part of that thinking makes sense. Charity work really is important. But just because the social value of your work may not be obvious, that doesn't mean it isn't there. You might just need to look at the bigger picture. If you struggle to find meaning in your work, step back, look at the big picture, and ask yourself, *How does my job help others? How does the work I do make the work of others possible? How does my work add to the common good of society?*

- *Work should be productive.* Your work should accomplish something, or at least help something get accomplished.

  This is easier to see in some jobs than in others. For example, if you're a carpenter and you build a bookshelf, you can see that shelf take shape and you can see when it's complete. If you work in an office and stare at a computer all day, it might be harder to understand what your work produces. Productivity, though, just like meaning, has a lot more to do with you than it does with the actual work you are doing. Chances are, if you work hard, challenge yourself, and work with skill, you will find your work to

"IF YOU DON'T CARE
ABOUT YOUR WORK, AND
IF YOU NEVER MAKE IT
ANY KIND OF PRIORITY IN
YOUR LIFE, IT'S PROBABLY
GOING TO LEAVE YOU
FEELING UNSATISFIED
AND FRUSTRATED."

be productive. If you're just doing the bare minimum and going through the motions, you probably won't. That's up to you.

- *Work should be fulfilling.* While your identity should never be overly tied up in your work, your work should bring you some level of satisfaction. This really gets to why you work and the expectations you have about your work.

  If you expect too much from your work—if you make work the most important thing in your life and expect it to always make you happy and make you feel important—then you are going to be let down. On the other hand, if you don't care about your work and if you never make it any kind of priority in your life, it's probably going to leave you feeling unsatisfied and frustrated.

  You have to find a balance. You can't make it ultimate in your life, but work should be an important part of a healthy, balanced life.

SO, HOW'S YOUR JOB?

Ask yourself this: A*m I settled in my work, or is there some unrest and inner noise?* If the latter is true, here are some common culprits.

- It could be that you expect your job to do something it was never intended to do, such as provide your identity or your ultimate security. *False assumptions about work can cause inner noise.*
- It could be that you give too much of your life to work. If this is the case, you are likely not only placing too great an emphasis on work, but you are also likely paying too little attention to other things that matter. *Overworking can cause inner noise.*

+ It could be that you give too little of your passion to your work. If you're just mailing it in and your heart isn't in it, it's probably time to step up your game. *Underworking can cause inner noise.*

+ It could be that your job doesn't fit your calling and gifts. If you're miserable in your work and you've been miserable for a long time, and you've really made an effort to make it work, then it may be time to make a change. There's nothing wrong with that. *The wrong fit or calling can cause inner noise.*

Be strategic about your work life. Sure, you may occasionally indulge in a daydream about an early retirement where you spend your days swinging a golf club or swinging in a hammock. But if you make that daydream a reality, or if you work in a way that isn't as fulfilling and productive as it could be, you'll be sorry just like my investment banker friend was. Deep inside, you'll realize that you fell short in an important part of the way you were made by your Creator.

Make changes in your life if you need to so that you quiet the inner noise that's drowning out your satisfaction in your work. (And as you can imagine, that change may not make a lot of sense from the standpoint of those who always equate making more money with feeling more fulfilled.) Think about what excites you and about what you uniquely have to offer. Then think about how to structure your life so that you're giving the best that is in you.

Don't let this slide. Take charge. Keep your passion for productivity alive. Manage your life so that work takes its rightful place in all that you do.

Remember this: The world needs what you have to offer through your energy, vision, and talents. And whether you feel it right now or not, you need to offer it.

1. Am I passionate and fully engaged in my work, or is it a half-hearted ritual or lifeless treadmill?
2. Am I operating in my sweet spot—within the area of my best skills?
3. Has burnout or boredom defined my recent work life? Am I as hardworking as I've been in the past?
4. Would my internal and external customers give my work strong, consistent scores?
5. Do I see the work of my hands as valuable, productive, and fulfilling?
6. Am I taking the initiative to sharpen my skill set and maintain excellence?

1. If you haven't been bringing your A game to work lately, then it's time to suit up and deliver your best effort. Don't just bring your body; bring your heart and soul, emotions and intellect.

2. If you're miserable in your work and have been for a long time, consider a career or job change. There's nothing wrong with that. According to a recent Forbes article, today's college graduates will have fifteen to twenty jobs over the course of their working lives.[14] It is remarkable how many workers in the United States are in a career unrelated to their college major.

3. If you've become too self-oriented in your work, find a cause that benefits others and lights a spark within you, and begin working there. Give back. Invest your skills and passion in something that doesn't have you at the center.

CHAPTER 8

CHOICE 3: WILL YOU KEEP YOUR LIFE IN BALANCE?

DURING A EUROPEAN vacation some years ago, my family and I were in Covent Garden, near London's theater district. The streets bustled with the activity of outdoor markets, vendors, and eateries. Street entertainers vied for an audience. A couple of guys playing guitars entertained tourists, while several violinists serenaded another group of onlookers. Children pounded on drums and actors performed skits. But to me, the most fascinating and colorful of all the entertainers were the jugglers.

One juggler, in his quest to outdo the others, had strung a tightrope between two columns about eight feet off the ground. As the crowd pressed in around him, he began stepping across the high wire, juggling knives, sticks, and bowling pins as he went. Then, to seal the crowd's interest, he added burning sticks to his performance! Either act—the high-wire walking or the juggling—would have been precarious enough, but to see this fellow performing both at once was amazing.

Michael Moschen, one of the world's greatest jugglers, claims that anyone can learn the art. "It's about breaking down complex patterns and maneuvers into simple tasks," he says. "Juggling is a system of tosses and throws, of different patterns that, once broken down, understood, and mastered, can be put together to create something magical."[15]

Easy for him to say!

When we're talking about all of the key tasks and relationships we're responsible for in life, is it really possible to juggle and keep our balance at the same time—to walk the tightrope and still keep all the knives and bowling pins from crashing down?

THE PHYSICS OF BALANCE

For better or worse, life is made up of moving parts that we constantly have to organize according to our available resources. It comes down to juggling multiple objects—objects that often change their size and weight in midair. Doing it well is a prime skill to learn if we're going to be successful in our own lives, experiencing the vitality and fulfillment we crave.

Think of it this way: Balance is the ability to juggle the assignments and opportunities of life. And what are these? *Assignments* are things we have no control over or cannot say no to. *Opportunities* are options that present themselves along the way—alternatives we can accept or decline.

A few years ago, I reached a point in my consulting business where my client list was growing, the staff I had to hire kept getting larger, and my schedule kept getting fuller. Talk about juggling! Every day, I had to make sure that a large number of high-capability business leaders were receiving the attention they wanted and deserved. It sometimes seemed I was going night and day. I hadn't reached the point of burnout yet, but I could see it peeking over the horizon.

And it wasn't just a matter of being too busy. I felt useful to the executives and managers who were coming to me, but I wanted to make an even more lasting impact in this world. Maybe in part it was because I was moving into middle age, but in any case, more and more I was thinking about what I could do for the next generation.

Before the pins fell to the floor, I resolved to upgrade my personal juggling act. Gradually I pared back my assignments with my consulting clients, shrinking and simplifying my company in the process. I also started offering myself to consult with a handful of young-gun social entrepreneurs who are out to make a big difference in the world. For me, at this point in my life, this feels like a much better life balance.

Have you stopped to consider what an effective life balance could mean for you? It's the key to becoming not just hardworking but hardworking for a point—to reach your fullest and widest potential.

There are two things to keep in mind when pursuing balance in life and work.

First, balance is not a one-time achievement. As much as we might like it to be, a balanced life is not a herculean effort of sorting priorities and then mindlessly executing the rest of your life. No tightrope walker suspends his walk in the middle and says, "I have done it." No, life requires us to walk forward every new day, facing whatever comes our way.

Second, balance is not the ability to do everything for everybody all the time. It's a skill for achieving the optimal, not the maximal. There are only so many items that even the world's greatest juggler can keep in the air at the same time.

IT STARTS WITH AWARENESS

If you don't know where you are, it's hard to maintain equilibrium. One leadership guru says, "Most people struggle with life balance simply because they haven't paid the price to decide what is really important to them."[16] A life of balance, therefore, begins with an awareness of all the facets of your life and the impact they have on you. It begins with the recognition of …

+ what you *are* involved in,
+ what you *could be* involved in, and
+ what you *should be* involved in.

Many people get so out of balance that they literally have to sell their businesses, quit their jobs, or take lengthy sabbaticals to think about what went wrong. They take such drastic steps to ensure that, once they return to the heat of the battle, they don't get out of balance again.

Ironically, many people who try to solve their balance problem with a sabbatical end up resigning shortly after they return to work. Why is that? Executive development consultant Caryn Joseph Siegel gives her answer: "I think it's because once they get away from the addiction of the work, they realize how nuts it was, and they don't want to live that way anymore."[17]

You can avoid such extreme measures if you pay closer attention to what's happening in your everyday life. It doesn't always take a month in a mountain cabin to get a handle on life. Scheduling regular times of quiet evaluation with your spouse, spending an hour every other week with a trusted advisor, or having a scheduled "day away" can do the trick.

What about you? How will you keep going, thriving not just for a season but for the long term? Balancing, rebalancing, then rebalancing again—that's one key way. One signal of greatness is people who dust themselves off after they fall and get back on the rope for another try.

"MOST PEOPLE
STRUGGLE WITH LIFE
BALANCE SIMPLY
BECAUSE THEY HAVEN'T
PAID THE PRICE TO
DECIDE WHAT IS
REALLY IMPORTANT
TO THEM."

1. Is my life in rhythm, with days of work, days of rest, and days of play?
2. Am I sleeping well?
3. Does one of my children particularly need me in this season of life?
4. How's the romance in my marriage?
5. Do I need a day away to realign my life?
6. Am I living a driven life or a called life?
7. Can I ever lay down my work?

1. If you don't have a hobby, get one.
2. If it seems that your best self-improvement efforts never stick, hire a coach.
3. Take a Sabbath rest each week. Turn off your cell phone and move away from the computer. Slow down and rest.
4. Review your work demands. Can you delegate better? Is there another structure that would help you achieve a better life balance and feel fulfillment?

CHAPTER 9

CHOICE 4: WILL YOU NURTURE QUALITY RELATIONSHIPS?

SOME TIME AGO I was coaching Roger, an executive within a Fortune 100 company who had decided to leave his high-paying job and start his own business. During the planning stage, Roger realized how much the success of his new venture hinged on some of his existing relationships—relationships that weren't all in tip-top shape. So he began what I called Operation Mend and Repair, an intentional effort to square things with the people he had worked with for more than twenty years before he left.

It didn't work. At least not at first.

People easily spotted his insincerity. They knew Roger had a selfish motive, and they wrote him off. He found it wasn't so easy to repair decades of failure to nurture healthy relationships. He had to actually change his ways of getting along with these people, rather than just buy a few cups of coffee for them, before the relationship-mending process finally succeeded.

Most of life winds back around to relationships. It takes a community to make it through life. Or as Anthony Robbins says, "The quality of your life is the quality of your relationships."

We were never intended to live isolated lives in which no one truly knows us. There's a lot to be said for having a Band of Brothers or a Ya-Ya Sisterhood. I know these are somewhat dated phrases, but here's the deal: the concept of having a close-knit, highly productive circle of friends is not new. Three thousand years ago, King Solomon urged us to secure that kind of circle.

It's better to have a partner than go it alone.
Share the work, share the wealth.
And if one falls down, the other helps,

But if there's no one to help, tough!

Two in a bed warm each other.
Alone, you shiver all night.

By yourself you're unprotected.
With a friend you can face the worst.
Can you round up a third?
A three-stranded rope isn't easily snapped.[18]

BUCKING THE TREND

Relationships are a part of a well-balanced flourishing life.
Yet American society seems to have steadily trended toward
individualism over the last half-century, and this tendency has
shown itself in how we work, in how we live, and even in the
words we use.

Did you know that in the last fifty or so years, the use of
individualistic words and phrases in books has significantly
increased, while the use of communal words and phrases
has decreased? Phrases such as "I come first" and "I can do
it myself" have become increasingly prevalent, while words
and phases such as "united" and "band together" have become
increasingly rare.

While this shift in vocabulary may not sound like a terribly
significant issue in itself, many wonder if it indicates a more
serious problem. Author David Brooks explains it like this:

> Over the past half-century, society has become more
> individualistic. As it has become more individualistic, it
> has also become less morally aware, because social and
> moral fabrics are inextricably linked. …

These gradual shifts in language reflect tectonic shifts in culture. We write less about community bonds and obligations because they're less central to our lives.[19]

To put it another way, we are better—better individuals, better workers, better parents, better citizens—when we live in community. When we live in isolation, and our focus and energies are solely on ourselves, we are simply less.

BECOMING A GIVER

Most of us develop our relationship styles early in life, and we generally fall into one of two categories—givers or takers. Vicente, an executive I know, had taker tendencies but he learned to be a giver.

When Vicente joined the board of a nonprofit in his community that offers leg-up services for the poor, he envisioned reading occasional reports and showing up for a few meetings each year. He believed in the organization's work in an arm's-length kind of way. The fact that his board service would look good on his CV had something to do with his joining too.

It came as a shock to Vicente when the chair insisted that the board members spend occasional weekends at the nonprofit's main facility in a run-down part of the city. Soon Vicente found himself sharing a room with a couple of other men from the board and taking his meals with homeless people fresh from the streets. *Why should I be spending my free time with these people?* Vicente grumbled to himself.

But thrown together with others in this way, he grew close to some of them, in particular one other man on the board—a lawyer-turned-convict-turned-social-activist who had a fascinating personality and endless stories to tell.

This friend converted Vicente's heart to the cause he was already a part of. In the process Vicente became a more fascinating person himself, somehow more full of life than before. And it was all the result of a genuine mutual friendship.

The simple fact is that relationships are important to successful leaders. And we all can improve our people skills. Improvement starts with recognizing the value of relationships, being willing to invest in people, and growing a few key relationships.

Are you ready for it? Start with the people closest to you—your family. Make it a priority, in addition, to develop your relationships with the people you work with most regularly as well as one or more friends who don't have any connection to your work at all (people like Vicente's ex-con activist pal). Real friendships require mutual interest, respect, and chemistry. Remember, this isn't primarily about what others can do for you. The relationships matter in themselves. And they matter to you because of what they mean to who you are and who you are becoming.

Nurturing relationships is a discipline you need to turn into a habit if you want to become a person with a rich and rewarding life.

"WE ARE BETTER—
BETTER INDIVIDUALS,
BETTER WORKERS,
BETTER PARENTS,
BETTER CITIZENS—
WHEN WE LIVE IN
COMMUNITY."

1. Do I tend to role-play in my relationships, not being honest, transparent, and vulnerable with those I call my friends?
2. Do I need to repair or refresh any relationships?
3. Do I really have a Band of Brothers or a Ya-Ya Sisterhood?
4. Am I investing in personal community and relationships?

1. Make a list of three people you think you could have deep, transparent, meaningful relationships with. Take a chance and try to strengthen the fabric of these friendships. Lean in a little—ask questions that will form a deeper connection.
2. Pick at least one friend and openly ask whether this person has an interest in dialing up the relational bond. Be ready with some ideas about how to spend quality time together.

CHAPTER 10

CHOICE 5: WILL YOU PURSUE SPIRITUAL VITALITY?

A BRILLIANT YOUNG academic—the kind of professor whom students clamor to hear—thought for many years that living for sex, friendship, and career success was all he needed. But he realized over time that he had a spiritual hunger inside. His dissatisfaction drove him eventually to seek out God. And when he sought, he found.

His name was Augustine, a fifth-century figure from North Africa best known today as a theologian and writer. His own experience led him to write these famous words about the spiritual hunger inside all humanity: "Thou madest us for Thyself, and our heart is restless, until it repose in Thee."[20]

Without question, there is a spiritual side to life. We might not all agree on the essentials of faith or how that faith ought to be expressed, but the importance of having faith in God or living out some kind of spiritual life is almost universally understood. Teilhard de Chardin, French philosopher and Jesuit priest, put it this way: "We are not human beings having a spiritual experience; we are spiritual beings having a human experience."[21]

One essential to successful self-management, leading to a life that yields satisfaction rather than regret, has got to be recognizing and cultivating your spirituality.

THE SPIRITUAL BUSINESSPERSON

For business leaders, in particular, it is tempting to lead a compartmentalized life. *Over here is my work life; over there is my family life*, a businessperson might think. I've got one set of ethics for my personal relationships and another when it comes to business. *I go to church on Sunday but my Christian identity counts for little during the rest of the week.*

But the nature of true spirituality is that it cannot be genuinely compartmentalized.

If God is your Creator and had a purpose for putting you on this earth at this time with the particular set of gifts and opportunities you possess, then your goal should be living for His will, wouldn't you say? If you claim to be a person of faith and mean it, then that's not just a style choice like the songs you download to your playlist. Instead, *it's who you are.* The morality and choices that are inherent in your beliefs ought to rule your life as a businessperson, family member, and citizen.

Among the titles I've given myself, one is *pragmatic theologian.* Some might think that odd for someone who advises business leaders and executives in complex strategy. I don't think so. We all have a theology that guides our lives. Some of us have formalized it or found language to define it. Others are simply living it out day by day in our choices. Time and again, I've dealt with unhappy executives and managers and have traced at least a part of their problem to a failure to integrate faith into their lives. Helping them find effective ways to let their spiritual natures bubble up and overflow into everything they do can often bring the coherence and alignment to life they deeply yearn for.

THE SYNERGY OF LEADERSHIP AND SPIRITUALITY

I remember having a breakfast meeting with Bill Pollard, then CEO of ServiceMaster Corporation, who said to me, "It's being involved in the rigor of the business world day in and day out that keeps my life of faith strong." After musing on that, I think I understood what he meant. The pressure, demands, and choices endemic to business require a transparency and authenticity in our faith not found in the routine of religion.

So you might find that unleashing your spirituality makes you a better organizational leader. And conversely, you might find that being an organizational leader helps you in your spirituality, if you'll let it. Both qualities—your leadership and your spirituality—are not only compatible but can mutually reinforce one another.

Don't ignore your spiritual side. Don't be afraid of it either. Cultivate it and let it thrive.

1. Do I enter the arena of the spiritual, or have I declared it a high-risk, don't-touch zone?
2. What is the condition of my heart, and how am I doing in regard to the unique temptations that leaders face?
3. Are prayer and Scripture reading the regular pattern of my life?
4. Am I integrating my faith into the details of my work?
5. What was the last transformational encounter I had with God?

1. Find a biography of a powerful leader who seemed to have a spiritual approach to life. Wade through his or her story, looking for what kept this person centered.
2. Read through the book of Proverbs in the Old Testament. Try to identify as many different personalities and kinds of people in it as you can. Use this exercise to expand your understanding and skill in leading different kinds of people.
3. Write out a prayer that captures all the things you're grateful for and anything that's weighing heavy on your heart.

CHAPTER 11

CHOICE 6: WILL YOU BE A STEWARD OF YOUR FINANCES?

ONE CHRISTMAS, I had a discussion with a married couple, both doctors, who had discovered that each of them would be getting a sizable year-end bonus plus a significant raise. They told me they were taking the month to ponder investing their extra money in worthy causes. In other words, they were planning to give it away. Frankly, it blew my mind! Most of us figure that the money we make belongs to us and that we have not only the right but maybe even the responsibility to consume it all ourselves.

This couple understood a great truth—that their attitude about money was more important than the money itself. They understood the importance of earning money honestly, holding it loosely, and using it wisely.

What about you?

EVERY WAY YOU TOUCH YOUR MONEY

Money has a way of connecting with so much else in our lives. So when you're looking for satisfaction in your life, ask yourself, *How am I doing with money?*

My point is not that you simply should be giving more money away, although that may be true. Rather, my point is that you need to know how to handle all aspects of money.

+ *Earning it.* Are you earning your money by working in your zone? Have you figured out your real value proposition, and are you charging at that level?

+ *Spending it.* Instead of giving in to the lure of more-more-more consumerism, are you making smart purchases that serve a real purpose in your life and that of your family?

+ *Saving and investing it.* Are you positioning some of your money to prepare for the challenges and opportunities the future will bring?

- *Giving it away.* Have you thought about how much to give away, and to what cause? Is your charitable giving strategic, so that it's returning real social or spiritual value? Are you realizing a 3BL or 4BL (three or four bottom line) ROI in your gifts or investments?[22]

If you're thinking about your money as an asset that God is asking you to steward for Him, I would suggest that all the areas above, and not just giving, are a part of that stewardship.

I will say, though, that giving is the area where people can get hung up in their money management. They think, *I work so hard for my money, why should I give it away?* They're worried that they'll be sacrificing their own happiness by giving some of their money away. In fact, the more money they have, the more they want. How well does that work for them?

In 2012, Forbes ran an article titled, "How Much Money Do You Really Need to Be Happy?" The article makes the point that, once you have the basic necessities of life covered, the amount of money you make doesn't have much to do with your level of happiness. People who made $55,000 annually were only 9 percent more content than people who made $25,000 a year.[23] (I'm not sure how you can be 9 percent more content, but you get the idea.) Furthermore, a 2008 LiveScience study found that people who gave away a portion of their bonuses were happier than people who spent those bonuses on themselves.[24]

So relax a little. Loosen your grip on your money. You can be happy and fulfilled while taking a more detached approach to your money—earning, spending, saving, investing, and giving it away not only for your own good but also for the good of others.

"FINANCIAL GIVING
IS SIMPLY ONE ASPECT
OF A GENEROUS
LIFESTYLE, A
LIFESTYLE THAT LOOKS
AT OUR TIME, TALENTS,
AND RESOURCES AS
TOOLS TO BETTER
THE LIVES OF THOSE
AROUND US. "

THE GENEROSITY LIFESTYLE

The impact of giving goes far beyond mere happiness. I firmly believe, and have witnessed over and over again, the simple but profound truth that *generous giving transforms the giver*. It changes the way we view ourselves, the way we view others, and what we hold dearly…all for the better.

The other struggle we tend to encounter related to giving is more practical in nature. *We don't know how to give well.* We know that giving is important. We know that we should be doing it. We even want to do it. But we don't know how. How much? How often? To what cause? What person? What organization?

While certainly important, in many ways these are the wrong questions, or at least the wrong place to start.

Giving well isn't about exact dollar amounts or percentages of income, and it isn't about choosing one cause or group over another. When rightly conceived, financial giving is simply one aspect of a generous lifestyle, a lifestyle that looks at our time, talents, and resources as tools to better the lives of those around us. When we start to think like this, we can give generously regardless of what is (or isn't) in our bank accounts.

MANAGING YOUR MONEY, MANAGING YOURSELF

As a part of managing yourself, you need to think through what money does and does not mean to your identity. You need to be cognizant and purposeful about every aspect of your personal finances. Only then will you build a balanced, flourishing life that you can look back on with profound satisfaction.

The two doctors I mentioned offer a good model. They didn't just give money away. They also worked hard in the profession they loved to make their money. They were using it to take good care of their family. They didn't too closely identify their personal worth with their net worth. They did the due diligence to figure out what was the best way to use their money for their loved ones and for others.

They were some of the happiest people I know, and they would still have been even if they made less money than they did. You can have that same kind of happiness if you'll make money your servant rather than letting money rule over you.

1. How tightly am I holding on to the money I earn?
2. When it comes to my financial life, where am I being diligent and where am I being lackadaisical?
3. Do I need to create a list of personal priorities or operating principles to guide my finances?
4. Is my personal contentment with what I have increasing or decreasing?
5. What was the last financial gift I made that brought me great joy?

1. Find a cause or a person that you deem worthy, and secretly invest there.
2. Take a look at your financial picture and identify the lifestyle you want to build. In other words, how much income is enough, before you're willing to start saving and giving in a big way?
3. Get a handle on your consumer spending and debt. Dream a bit about how you might leverage your assets for the greatest ROI.
4. Do an audit on all your investments and gifts to determine which of them are high impact and multiple bottom line.

CONCLUSION

LIFE DOESN'T COME with an Undo or Back key. Our actions have consequences, and often we cannot reverse those consequences. If you neglect your spouse, you may not be able to save your marriage. If you lie on your year-end financials, you may lose your business partners. If you suffer an ethical failing, you may be disqualified from ministry. These are hard truths, but truths nonetheless. If you've made mistakes, ruined relationships, and ended up in the ditch, you can't change that. What you can do is pick yourself up, make some changes and ensure that you get out of the ditch, and try to never end up there again.

No matter how old you are, or how set in your ways you have been, it's never too late to make changes. It's never too late to prevent future failings, collapses, and the regret that comes with them.

That's the point of *Managing Me*. We've all burned up some resources, never to get them back, but we also all have the chance to be better moving forward, to live a balanced, flourishing life. We can begin to make a habit of paying attention to our own choices and deciding which habits to inculcate in our lives.

Ignatius of Loyola, founder of the Jesuits—the original company that I mentioned in Chapter 2—urged his followers to practice the daily examen. That is, at night before going to bed, they were to think back over their day, be grateful for the good things that had occurred, and think about how to improve where they had made mistakes. It was a key part of the Jesuits' self-management.

I'm not urging you specifically to following the Ignatian *examen*. But I am urging you to be self-aware and self-directive regarding your choices. If you're a leader, start with leading yourself. This will not only produce improvement in your work performance, benefiting others, but also makes it possible for you to look back on your whole life at the end and feel a contentment about what you were able to accomplish.

Socrates once said, "Let him that would move the world, first move himself." Start by managing yourself—and who knows what you will achieve!

"LET HIM THAT WOULD
MOVE THE WORLD,
FIRST MOVE HIMSELF."
– SOCRATES

SUPPORTING
SCRIPTURES

*(from the Holman Christian
Standard Bible)*

It is up to me to manage me. I cannot outsource it or ignore it. Keep an eye on the little things.

2 Samuel 11-12—In the spring when kings march out to war, David sent Joab with his officers and all Israel. They destroyed the Ammonites and besieged Rabbah, but David remained in Jerusalem. One evening David got up from his bed and strolled around on the roof of the palace. From the roof he saw a woman bathing—a very beautiful woman. So David sent someone to inquire about her, and he reported, "This is Bathsheba, daughter of Eliam and wife of Uriah the Hittite."

David sent messengers to get her, and when she came to him, he slept with her. Now she had just been purifying herself from her uncleanness. Afterward, she returned home. The woman conceived and sent word to inform David: "I am pregnant." David sent orders to Joab: "Send me Uriah the Hittite." So Joab sent Uriah to David. When Uriah came to him, David asked how Joab and the troops were doing and how the war was going. 8 Then he said to Uriah, "Go down to your house and wash your feet." So Uriah left the palace, and a gift from the king followed him. But Uriah slept at the door of the palace with all his master's servants; he did not go down to his house.

When it was reported to David, "Uriah didn't go home," David questioned Uriah, "Haven't you just come from a journey? Why didn't you go home?" Uriah answered David, "The ark, Israel, and Judah are dwelling in tents, and my master Joab and his soldiers are camping in the open field. How can I enter my house to eat and drink and sleep with my wife? As surely as you live and by your life, I will not do this!"

"Stay here today also," David said to Uriah, "and tomorrow I will send you back." So Uriah stayed in Jerusalem that day and the next. Then David invited Uriah to eat and drink with him, and David got him drunk. He went out in the evening to lie down on his cot with his master's servants, but he did not go home.

The next morning David wrote a letter to Joab and sent it with Uriah. In the letter he wrote:

Put Uriah at the front of the fiercest fighting, then withdraw from him so that he is struck down and dies.

When Joab was besieging the city, he put Uriah in the place where he knew the best enemy soldiers were. Then the men of the city came out and attacked Joab, and some of the men from David's soldiers fell in battle; Uriah the Hittite also died.

Joab sent someone to report to David all the details of the battle. He commanded the messenger, "When you've finished telling the king all the details of the battle—if the king's anger gets stirred up and he asks you, 'Why did you get so close to the city to fight? Didn't you realize they would shoot from the top of the wall? At Thebez, who struck Abimelech son of Jerubbesheth? Didn't a woman drop an upper millstone on him from the top of the wall so that he died? Why did you get so close to the wall?'—then say, 'Your servant Uriah the Hittite is dead also.'" Then the messenger left.

When he arrived, he reported to David all that Joab had sent him to tell. The messenger reported to David, "The men gained the advantage over us and came out against us in the field, but we counterattacked right up to the entrance of the gate. However, the archers shot down on your soldiers from the top of the wall, and some of the king's soldiers died. Your servant Uriah the Hittite is also dead."

David told the messenger, "Say this to Joab: 'Don't let this matter upset you because the sword devours all alike. Intensify your fight against the city and demolish it.' Encourage him."

When Uriah's wife heard that her husband Uriah had died, she mourned for him. When the time of mourning ended, David had her brought to his house. She became his wife and bore him a son. However, the Lord considered what David had done to be evil.

Chapter 12

So the Lord sent Nathan to David. When he arrived, he said to him:

There were two men in a certain city, one rich and the other poor. The rich man had a large number of sheep and cattle, but the poor man had nothing except one small ewe lamb that he had bought. He raised it, and it grew up, living with him and his children. It shared his meager food and drank from his cup; it slept in his arms, and it was like a daughter to him. Now a traveler came to the rich man, but the rich man could not bring himself to take one of his own sheep or cattle to prepare for the traveler who had come to him. Instead, he took the poor man's lamb and prepared it for his guest.

David was infuriated with the man and said to Nathan: "As the Lord lives, the man who did this deserves to die! Because he has done this thing and shown no pity, he must pay four lambs for that lamb."

Nathan replied to David, "You are the man! This is what the Lord God of Israel says: 'I anointed you king over Israel, and I delivered you from the hand of Saul. I gave your master's house to you and your master's wives into your arms, and I gave you the house of Israel and Judah, and if that was not enough, I would have given you even more. Why then have you despised the command of the Lord by doing what I consider evil? You struck down Uriah the Hittite with the sword and took his wife as your own wife—you murdered him with the Ammonite's sword. Now therefore, the sword will never leave your house because you despised Me and took the wife of Uriah the Hittite to be your own wife.'

"This is what the Lord says, 'I am going to bring disaster on you from your own family: I will take your wives and give them to another before your very eyes, and he will sleep with them publicly. You acted in secret, but I will do this before all Israel and in broad daylight.'"

David responded to Nathan, "I have sinned against the Lord."

Then Nathan replied to David, "The Lord has taken away your sin; you will not die. However, because you treated the Lord with such contempt in this matter, the son born to you will die." Then Nathan went home.

The Lord struck the baby that Uriah's wife had borne to David, and he became ill. David pleaded with God for the boy. He fasted, went home, and spent the night lying on the ground. The elders of his house stood beside him to get him up from the ground, but he was unwilling and would not eat anything with them.

On the seventh day the baby died. But David's servants were afraid to tell him the baby was dead. They said, "Look, while the baby was alive, we spoke to him, and he wouldn't listen to us. So how can we tell him the baby is dead? He may do something desperate."

When David saw that his servants were whispering to each other, he guessed that the baby was dead. So he asked his servants, "Is the baby dead?"

"He is dead," they replied.

Then David got up from the ground. He washed, anointed himself, changed his clothes, went to the Lord's house, and worshiped. Then he went home and requested something to eat. So they served him food, and he ate.

His servants asked him, "What did you just do? While the baby was alive, you fasted and wept, but when he died, you got up and ate food."

He answered, "While the baby was alive, I fasted and wept because I thought, 'Who knows? The Lord may be gracious to me and let him live.' But now that he is dead, why should I fast? Can I bring him back again? I'll go to him, but he will never return to me."

Then David comforted his wife Bathsheba; he went and slept with her. She gave birth to a son and named him Solomon. The Lord loved him, and He sent a message through Nathan the prophet, who named him Jedidiah, because of the Lord.

1 Corinthians 9:24-27—Don't you know that the runners in a stadium all race, but only one receives the prize? Run in such a way to win the prize. Now everyone who competes exercises self-control in everything. However, they do it to receive a crown that will fade away, but we a crown that will never fade away. Therefore I do not run like one who runs aimlessly or box like one beating the air. Instead, I discipline my body and bring it under strict control, so that after preaching to others, I myself will not be disqualified.

2 Timothy 2:1-6—You, therefore, my son, be strong in the grace that is in Christ Jesus. And what you have heard from me in the presence of many witnesses, commit to faithful men who will be able to teach others also. Share in suffering as a good soldier of Christ Jesus. No one serving as a soldier gets entangled in the concerns of civilian life; he seeks to please the recruiter. Also, if anyone competes as an athlete, he is not crowned unless he competes according to the rules. The hardworking farmer ought to be the first to get a share of the crops.

Daniel 1—In the third year of the reign of Jehoiakim king of Judah, Nebuchadnezzar king of Babylon came to Jerusalem and laid siege to it. The Lord handed Jehoiakim king of Judah over to him, along with some of the vessels from the house of God. Nebuchadnezzar carried them to the land of Babylon, to the house of his god, and put the vessels in the treasury of his god.

The king ordered Ashpenaz, the chief of his court officials, to bring some of the Israelites from the royal family and from the nobility—young men without any physical defect, good-looking, suitable for instruction in all wisdom, knowledgeable, perceptive, and capable of serving in the king's palace—and to teach them the Chaldean language and literature. The king assigned them daily provisions from the royal food and from the wine that he drank. They were to be trained for three years, and at the end of that time they were to serve in the king's court. Among them, from the descendants of Judah, were Daniel, Hananiah, Mishael, and Azariah. The chief official gave them other names: he gave the name Belteshazzar to Daniel, Shadrach to Hananiah, Meshach to Mishael, and Abednego to Azariah.

Daniel determined that he would not defile himself with the king's food or with the wine he drank. So he asked permission from the chief official not to defile himself. God had granted Daniel favor and compassion from the chief official, yet he said to Daniel, "My lord the king assigned your food and drink. I'm afraid of what would happen if he saw your faces looking thinner than those of the other young men your age. You would endanger my life with the king."

So Daniel said to the guard whom the chief official had assigned to Daniel, Hananiah, Mishael, and Azariah, "Please test your servants for 10 days. Let us be given vegetables to eat and water to drink. Then examine our appearance and the appearance of the young men who are eating the king's food, and deal with your servants based on what you see." He agreed with them about this and tested them for 10 days. At the end of 10 days they looked better and healthier than all the young men who were eating the king's food. So the guard continued to remove their food and the wine they were to drink and gave them vegetables.

God gave these four young men knowledge and understanding in every kind of literature and wisdom. Daniel also understood visions and dreams of every kind. At the end of the time that the king had said to present them, the chief official presented them to Nebuchadnezzar. The king interviewed them, and among all of them, no one was found equal to Daniel, Hananiah, Mishael, and Azariah. So they began to serve in the king's court. In every matter of wisdom and understanding that the king consulted them about, he found them 10 times better than all the diviner-priests and mediums in his entire kingdom. Daniel remained there until the first year of King Cyrus.

A life with no regrets.

1 Corinthians 3:5-15—What then is Apollos? And what is Paul? They are servants through whom you believed, and each has the role the Lord has given. I planted, Apollos watered, but God gave the growth. So then neither the one who plants nor the one who waters is anything, but only God who gives the growth. Now the one planting and the one watering are one in purpose, and each will receive his own reward according to his own labor. For we are God's coworkers. You are God's field, God's building. According to God's grace that was given to me, I have laid a foundation as a skilled master builder, and another builds on it. But each one must be careful how he builds on it. For no one can lay any other foundation than what has been laid down. That foundation is Jesus Christ. If anyone builds on that foundation with gold, silver, costly stones, wood, hay, or straw, each one's work will become obvious, for the day will disclose it, because it will be revealed by fire; the fire will test the quality of each one's work. If anyone's work that he has built survives, he will receive a reward. If anyone's work is burned up, it will be lost, but he will be saved; yet it will be like an escape through fire.

Proverbs 25:28—A man who does not control his temper is like a city whose wall is broken down.

Choice 1—Will You Establish Strategic Clarity?

Luke 14:25-33—Now great crowds were traveling with Him. So He turned and said to them: "If anyone comes to Me and does not hate his own father and mother, wife and children, brothers and sisters—yes, and even his own life—he cannot be My disciple. Whoever does not bear his own cross and come after Me cannot be My disciple. For which of you, wanting to build a tower, doesn't first sit down and calculate the cost to see if he has enough to complete it? Otherwise, after he has laid the foundation and cannot finish it, all the onlookers will begin to make fun of him, saying, 'This man started to build and wasn't able to finish.' Or what king, going to war against another king, will not first sit down and decide if he is able with 10,000 to oppose the one who comes against him with 20,000? If not, while the other is still far off, he sends a delegation and asks for terms of peace. In the same way, therefore, every one of you who does not say good-bye to all his possessions cannot be My disciple.

Habakkuk 2:2—The Lord answered me: Write down this vision; clearly inscribe it on tablets so one may easily read it.

1 Thessalonians 5:21—But test all things. Hold on to what is good.

Psalm 90:12—Teach us to number our days carefully so that we may develop wisdom in our hearts.

Micah 6:8—Mankind, He has told you what is good and what it is the Lord requires of you: to act justly, to love faithfulness, and to walk humbly with your God.

Choice 2—Will You Make Your Contribution to the World?

2 Peter 1:5-9—For this very reason, make every effort to supplement your faith with goodness, goodness with knowledge, knowledge with self-control, self-control with endurance, endurance with godliness, godliness with brotherly affection, and brotherly affection with love. For if these qualities are yours and are increasing, they will keep you from being useless or unfruitful in the knowledge of our Lord Jesus Christ. The person who lacks these things is blind and shortsighted and has forgotten the cleansing from his past sins.

Psalm 127:1-2—Unless the Lord builds a house, its builders labor over it in vain; unless the Lord watches over a city, the watchman stays alert in vain. In vain you get up early and stay up late, working hard to have enough food—yes, He gives sleep to the one He loves.

Exodus 31:1-11—The Lord also spoke to Moses: "Look, I have appointed by name Bezalel son of Uri, son of Hur, of the tribe of Judah. I have filled him with God's Spirit, with wisdom, understanding, and ability in every craft to design artistic works in gold, silver, and bronze, to cut gemstones for mounting, and to carve wood for work in every craft. I have also selected Oholiab son of Ahisamach, of the tribe of Dan, to be with him. I have placed wisdom within every skilled craftsman in order to make all that I have commanded you: the tent of meeting, the ark of the testimony, the mercy seat that is on top of it, and all the other furnishings of the tent—the table with its utensils, the pure gold lampstand with all its utensils, the altar of incense, the altar of burnt offering with all its utensils, the basin with its stand— the specially woven garments, both the holy garments for Aaron the priest and the garments for his sons to serve as priests, the anointing oil, and the fragrant incense for the sanctuary. They must make them according to all that I have commanded you."

Colossians 3:22-24—Slaves, obey your human masters in everything. Don't work only while being watched, in order to please men, but work wholeheartedly, fearing the Lord. Whatever you do, do it enthusiastically, as something done for the Lord and not for men, knowing that you will receive the reward of an inheritance from the Lord. You serve the Lord Christ.

Choice 3—Will You Keep Your Life in Balance?

Exodus 18:1-27—Moses' father-in-law Jethro, the priest of Midian, heard about everything that God had done for Moses and His people Israel, and how the Lord had brought Israel out of Egypt. Now Jethro, Moses' father-in-law, had taken in Zipporah, Moses' wife, after he had sent her back, along with her two sons, one of whom was named Gershom (because Moses had said, "I have been a foreigner in a foreign land") and the other Eliezer (because he had said, "The God of my father was my helper and delivered me from Pharaoh's sword"). Moses' father-in-law Jethro, along with Moses' wife and sons, came to him in the wilderness where he was camped at the mountain of God. He sent word to Moses, "I, your father-in-law Jethro, am coming to you with your wife and her two sons."

So Moses went out to meet his father-in-law, bowed down, and then kissed him. They asked each other how they had been and went into the tent. Moses recounted to his father-in-law all that the Lord had done to Pharaoh and the Egyptians for Israel's sake, all the hardships that confronted them on the way, and how the Lord delivered them. Jethro rejoiced over all the good things the Lord had done for Israel when He rescued them from the power of the Egyptians. "Praise the Lord," Jethro exclaimed, "who rescued you from Pharaoh and the power of the Egyptians and snatched the people from the power of the Egyptians. Now I know that Yahweh is greater than all gods, because He did wonders when the Egyptians acted arrogantly against Israel." Then Jethro, Moses' father-in-law, brought a burnt offering and sacrifices to God, and Aaron came with all the elders of Israel to eat a meal with Moses' father-in-law in God's presence.

The next day Moses sat down to judge the people, and they stood around Moses from morning until evening. When Moses' father-in-law saw everything he was doing for them he asked, "What is this thing you're doing for the people? Why are you alone sitting as judge, while all the people stand around you from morning until evening?" Moses replied to his father-in-law, "Because the people come to me to inquire of God. Whenever they have a dispute, it comes to me, and I make a decision between one man and another. I teach them God's statutes and laws."

"What you're doing is not good," Moses' father-in-law said to him. "You will certainly wear out both yourself and these people who are with you, because the task is too heavy for you. You can't do it alone. Now listen to me; I will give you some advice, and God be with you. You be the one to represent the people before God and bring their cases to Him. Instruct them about the statutes and laws, and teach them the way to live and what they must do. But you should select from all the people able men, God-fearing, trustworthy, and hating bribes. Place them over the people as commanders of thousands, hundreds, fifties, and tens. They should judge the people at all times. Then they can bring you every important case but judge every minor case themselves. In this way you will lighten your load, and they will bear it with you. If you do this, and God so directs you, you will be able to endure, and also all these people will be able to go home satisfied."

Moses listened to his father-in-law and did everything he said. So Moses chose able men from all Israel and made them leaders over the people as commanders of thousands, hundreds, fifties, and tens. They judged the people at all times; they would bring the hard cases to Moses, but they would judge every minor case themselves. Then Moses said good-bye to his father-in-law, and he journeyed to his own land.

Luke 2:52—Jesus increased in wisdom and stature, and in favor with God and with people.

Ecclesiastes 3:1-8—There is an occasion for everything, and a time for every activity under heaven: a time to give birth and a time to die; a time to plant and a time to uproot; a time to kill and a time to heal; a time to tear down and a time to build; a time to weep and a time to laugh; a time to mourn and a time to dance; a time to throw stones and a time to gather stones; a time to embrace and a time to avoid embracing; a time to search and a time to count as lost; a time to keep and a time to throw away; a time to tear and a time to sew; a time to be silent and a time to speak; a time to love and a time to hate; a time for war and a time for peace.

Philippians 4:8—Finally, brothers, whatever is true, whatever is honorable, whatever is just, whatever is pure, whatever is lovely, whatever is commendable—if there is any moral excellence and if there is any praise—dwell on these things.

Colossians 3:17—And whatever you do, in word or in deed, do every-thing in the name of the Lord Jesus, giving thanks to God the Father through Him.

Psalm 127—Unless the Lord builds a house, its builders labor over it in vain; unless the Lord watches over a city, the watchman stays alert in vain. In vain you get up early and stay up late, working hard to have enough food—yes, He gives sleep to the one He loves. Sons are indeed a heritage from the Lord, children, a reward. Like arrows in the hand of a warrior are the sons born in one's youth. Happy is the man who has filled his quiver with them. Such men will never be put to shame when they speak with their enemies at the city gate.

Choice 4—Will You Nurture Quality Relationships?

Acts 2:42-47—And they devoted themselves to the apostles' teaching, to the fellowship, to the breaking of bread, and to the prayers. Then fear came over everyone, and many wonders and signs were being performed through the apostles. Now all the believers were together and held all things in common. They sold their possessions and property and distributed the proceeds to all, as anyone had a need. Every day they devoted themselves to meeting together in the temple complex, and broke bread from house to house. They ate their food with a joyful and humble attitude, praising God and having favor with all the people. And every day the Lord added to them those who were being saved.

Romans 12:4—Now as we have many parts in one body, and all the parts do not have the same function.

Ecclesiastes 4:9-12—Two are better than one because they have a good reward for their efforts. For if either falls, his companion can lift him up; but pity the one who falls without another to lift him up. Also, if two lie down together, they can keep warm; but how can one person alone keep warm? And if someone overpowers one person, two can resist him. A cord of three strands is not easily broken.

Proverbs 13:20—The one who walks with the wise will become wise, but a companion of fools will suffer harm.

Proverbs 17:17—A friend loves at all times, and a brother is born for a difficult time.

Proverbs 27:17—Iron sharpens iron, and one man sharpens another.

Hebrews 10:24—Let us be concerned about one another in order to promote love and good works.

Choice 5—Will You Pursue Spiritual Vitality?

Romans 12:1-2—Therefore, brothers, by the mercies of God, I urge you to present your bodies as a living sacrifice, holy and pleasing to God; this is your spiritual worship. Do not be conformed to this age, but be transformed by the renewing of your mind, so that you may discern what is the good, pleasing, and perfect will of God.

Philippians 4:8—Whatever is true, whatever is honorable, whatever is just, whatever is pure, whatever is lovely, whatever is commendable —if there is any moral excellence and if there is any praise—dwell on these things.

Colossians 3:16-17—Let the message about the Messiah dwell richly among you, teaching and admonishing one another in all wisdom, and singing psalms, hymns, and spiritual songs, with gratitude in your hearts to God. And whatever you do, in word or in deed, do everything in the name of the Lord Jesus, giving thanks to God the Father through Him.

Jeremiah 9:23-24—This is what the Lord says: The wise man must not boast in his wisdom; the strong man must not boast in his strength; the wealthy man must not boast in his wealth. But the one who boasts should boast in this, that he understands and knows Me—that I am Yahweh, showing faithful love, justice, and righteousness on the earth, for I delight in these things. This is the Lord's declaration.

John 15:1-17—"I am the true vine, and My Father is the vineyard keeper. Every branch in Me that does not produce fruit He removes, and He prunes every branch that produces fruit so that it will produce more fruit. You are already clean because of the word I have spoken to you. Remain in Me, and I in you. Just as a branch is unable to produce fruit by itself unless it remains on the vine, so neither can you unless you remain in Me.

"I am the vine; you are the branches. The one who remains in Me and I in him produces much fruit, because you can do nothing without Me. If anyone does not remain in Me, he is thrown aside like a branch and he withers. They gather them, throw them into the fire, and they are burned. If you remain in Me and My words remain in you, ask whatever you want and it will be done for you. My Father is glorified by this: that you produce much fruit and prove to be My disciples. "As the Father has loved Me, I have also loved you. Remain in My love. If you keep My commands you will remain in My love, just as I have kept My Father's commands and remain in His love.

"I have spoken these things to you so that My joy may be in you and your joy may be complete. This is My command: Love one another as I have loved you. No one has greater love than this, that someone would lay down his life for his friends. You are My friends if you do what I command you. I do not call you slaves anymore, because a slave doesn't know what his master is doing. I have called you friends, because I have made known to you everything I have heard from My Father. You did not choose Me, but I chose you. I appointed you that you should go out and produce fruit and that your fruit should remain, so that whatever you ask the Father in My name, He will give you. This is what I command you: Love one another."

Choice 6—Will You Be a Steward of Your Finances?

Malachi 3:6-12—"I, Yahweh, have not changed, you descendants of Jacob have not been destroyed. Since the days of your fathers, you have turned from My statutes; you have not kept them. Return to Me, and I will return to you," says the Lord of Hosts.

But you ask: "How can we return?"

"Will a man rob God? Yet you are robbing Me!"

You ask: "How do we rob You?"

"By not making the payments of the tenth and the contributions. You are suffering under a curse, yet you—the whole nation—are still robbing Me. Bring the full tenth into the storehouse so that there may be food in My house. Test Me in this way," says the Lord of Hosts. "See if I will not open the floodgates of heaven and pour out a blessing for you without measure. I will rebuke the devourer for you, so that it will not ruin the produce of your land and your vine in your field will not fail to produce fruit," says the Lord of Hosts. "Then all the nations will consider you fortunate, for you will be a delightful land," says the Lord of Hosts.

2 Corinthians 9:6-15—Remember this: The person who sows sparingly will also reap sparingly, and the person who sows generously will also reap generously. Each person should do as he has decided in his heart—not reluctantly or out of necessity, for God loves a cheerful giver. And God is able to make every grace overflow to you, so that in every way, always having everything you need, you may excel in every good work. As it is written:

He scattered;

He gave to the poor;

His righteousness endures forever.

Now the One who provides seed for the sower and bread for food will provide and multiply your seed and increase the harvest of your righteousness. You will be enriched in every way for all generosity, which produces thanksgiving to God through us. For the ministry of this service is not only supplying the needs of the saints, but is also overflowing in many acts of thanksgiving to God. They will glorify God for your obedience to the confession of the gospel of Christ, and for your generosity in sharing with them and with others through the proof provided by this service. And they will have deep affection for you in their prayers on your behalf because of the surpassing grace of God in you. Thanks be to God for His indescribable gift.

Ecclesiastes 5:10—The one who loves money is never satisfied with money, and whoever loves wealth is never satisfied with income. This too is futile.

Matthew 6:24—"No one can be a slave of two masters, since either he will hate one and love the other, or be devoted to one and despise the other. You cannot be slaves of God and of money."

1 Timothy 6:17-19—Instruct those who are rich in the present age not to be arrogant or to set their hope on the uncertainty of wealth, but on God, who richly provides us with all things to enjoy. Instruct them to do what is good, to be rich in good works, to be generous, willing to share, storing up for themselves a good reserve for the age to come, so that they may take hold of life that is real.

Matthew 25:14-30—"For it is just like a man going on a journey. He called his own slaves and turned over his possessions to them. To one he gave five talents; to another, two; and to another, one— to each according to his own ability. Then he went on a journey. Immediately the man who had received five talents went, put them to work, and earned five more. In the same way the man with two earned two more. But the man who had received one talent went off, dug a hole in the ground, and hid his master's money.

"After a long time the master of those slaves came and settled accounts with them. The man who had received five talents approached, presented five more talents, and said, 'Master, you gave me five talents. Look, I've earned five more talents.'

"His master said to him, 'Well done, good and faithful slave! You were faithful over a few things; I will put you in charge of many things. Share your master's joy!'

"Then the man with two talents also approached. He said, 'Master, you gave me two talents. Look, I've earned two more talents.'

"His master said to him, 'Well done, good and faithful slave! You were faithful over a few things; I will put you in charge of many things. Share your master's joy!'

"Then the man who had received one talent also approached and said, 'Master, I know you. You're a difficult man, reaping where you haven't sown and gathering where you haven't scattered seed. So I was afraid and went off and hid your talent in the ground. Look, you have what is yours.'

"But his master replied to him, 'You evil, lazy slave! If you knew that I reap where I haven't sown and gather where I haven't scattered, then you should have deposited my money with the bankers. And when I returned I would have received my money back with interest.

"'So take the talent from him and give it to the one who has 10 talents. For to everyone who has, more will be given, and he will have more than enough. But from the one who does not have, even what he has will be taken away from him. And throw this good-for-nothing slave into the outer darkness. In that place there will be weeping and gnashing of teeth.'"

NOTES

1. Christopher P. Neck and Charles C. Manz, "Self-Leadership: Leading Yourself to Personal Excellence," http://www.emergingleader.com/article4.shtml

2. Simon Sinek, Start with Why: How Great Leaders Inspire Everyone to Take Action (New York: Portfolio, 2009).

3. Daniel Goleman, "The Focused Leader." http://hbr.org/2013/12/the-focused-leader/ar/1.

4. John C. Maxwell, Developing the Leaders Around You: How to Help Others Reach Their Full Potential. (Nashville: Thomas Nelson, 2005), 20.

5. Samuel D. Rima, Leading from the Inside Out: The Art of Self-Leadership (Grand Rapids, MI: Baker, 2000), 27.

6. Stephen R. Covey. The Seven Habits of Highly Effective People: Restoring the Character Ethic (New York: Simon & Schuster, 1989).

7. Johann Wolfgang von Goethe quoted in The 7 Habits of Highly Effective Families. Stephen R. Covey (St. Martin's Griffin, 1998), 114.

8. Peter Drucker, Management Challenges for the 21st Century. 1999.

9. Alan L. Wurtzel. Good to Great to Gone: The 60-Year Rise and Fall of Circuit City (New York: Diversion Books, 2012).

10. Andy Stanley, The Principle of the Path: How to Get from Where You Are to Where You Want to Be (Nashville: Thomas Nelson, 2008), 150.

11. Charles Colson and Jack Eckerd. Why America Doesn't Work (Nashville: Thomas Nelson 1992).

12. Stephen Covey, The 8th Habit: From Effectiveness to Greatness (Free Press, 2004), 63.

13. 1 Thessalonians 4:11, NIV

14. Jeanne Meister. "Job Hopping Is the 'New Normal' for Millennials: Three Ways to Prevent a Human Resource Nightmare," Forbes, August 4, 2012, http://www.forbes.com/sites/jeannemeister/2012/08/14/job-hopping-is-the-new-normal-for-millennials-three-ways-to-prevent-a-human-resource-nightmare/.

15. Quoted in Anna Muoio, "Life Is a Juggling Act," Fast Company, October 31, 1997, http://www.fastcompany.com/33137/life-juggling-act.

16. Stephen Covey, interview by Kyra Phillips, CNN, January 9, 2003, http://edition.cnn.com/TRANSCRIPTS/0301/09/lol.02.html.

17. Quoted in Tony Schwartz, "Life/Work—Issue 34," Fast Company, April 30, 2000, http://www.fastcompany.com/39642/life-work-issue-34.

18. Ecclesiastes 4:9-12, The Message.

19. David Brooks, "What Our Words Tell Us," New York Times, May 20, 2013, http://www.nytimes.com/2013/05/21/opinion/brooks-what-our-words-tell-us.html?_r=1&.

20. Augustine, The Confessions of St. Augustine, trans. Edward B. Pusey, 26, http://www.ccel.org/ccel/augustine/confess.pdf.

21. Quoted in Stephen R. Covey, *Living the Seven Habits: Stories of Courage and Inspiration* (New York: Fireside, 2000), 47.

22. Stephen R. Graves, "The Defying Power of a MBL (Multiple Bottom Line)," June 2, 2014, http://www.stephenrgraves.com/mbl/.

23. Robert Glatter, M.D. "How Much Money Do You Really Need to Be Happy?" *Forbes,* July 27, 2012, http://www.forbes.com/sites/robertglatter/2012/07/27/how-much-money-do-you-need-to-be-happy-2/.

24. Jeanna Bryner. "Key to Happiness: Give Away Money," *LiveScience,* March 19, 2008, http://www.livescience.com/2376-key-happiness-give-money.html.

THE BUSINESS OF GENEROSITY:
How Companies, Nonprofits, and Churches are Working Together to Deliver Remarkable Good

In *The Business of Generosity* you will:

+ Learn what is driving young entrepreneurs to move beyond the single bottom line
+ Develop a framework for leading your company to stay profitable, do good and remain true to your mission all in harmony
+ Discover how churches, business and communities are working together to deliver remarkable good
+ Construct language to articulate the "why" of what you do
+ Become more intentional and strategic with the giving you do as a business and as an individual

MANAGING ME:
Why Some Leaders Build a Remarkable Legacy and Others Sadly Crumble

In *Managing Me* you will:
+ Better understand why self-leadership is so hard
+ Marry the ambition of leading your company and leading yourself
+ Be introduced to a model of sustainable leadership
+ Identify the critical gauges that steer your life and work progress
+ Create a filter to help sort the things that matter most

STRATEGY 3.0:

A Guide for Entrepreneurs, Millennials, Frustrated 5-year Planners and Anyone Else Searching for Fast, Focused, and Agile Strategy

In _Strategy 3.0_ you will:

+ Learn why operating in old frameworks from an outdated perspective is such a costly mistake for leaders
+ Improve your ability to pivot and take advantage of market opportunities
+ Set your next company horizon and feel confident about reaching it
+ Encounter the fifteen critical terms and phrases that have become the working vocabulary of fast yet adaptive strategy
+ Develop and refine an eye that can extract the insights that are the foundation of all effective strategy

FLOURISHING:
Why Some People Thrive and Others Just Survive

In *Flourishing* you will:

+ Learn how to balance the competing demands of life and work
+ Unearth eight insights that anchor those who flourish most
+ Discover the kind of life you were designed to enjoy
+ See the value of slowing down (and what to actually do when you slow down)
+ Identify your true voice—the sound that your life makes when operating in its strike zone

THE HERO LEADER:
Why Effective Leaders Combine Strengths and Weaknesses

In *The Hero Leader* you will:

+ Understand the seven collective skill sets that all great leaders and managers develop
+ Learn how to become a legacy leader that others love to follow
+ Pinpoint what your team needs to develop and to lift their leadership horizon
+ See the opposite side of your core strengths and what the dangers are of ignoring those weaknesses
+ Consider how to staff in light of your personal skill set

THE GOSPEL GOES TO WORK:
God's Big Canvas of Calling and Renewal

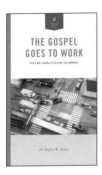

In *The Gospel Goes To Work* you will:

+ Learn how the reach, power and intent of the Gospel can transform any work
+ Discover that work is a center piece of God's creation and redemptive renewal
+ Get beyond the default view of evangelizing and moralizing being the highest expression of taking the gospel to work
+ Identify the universal Baselines of Gospel impressions for all work for every worker
+ Imagine the Blue Sky possibilities of Gospel impact in your particular work using your particular wiring

About Steve

Steve is the founder of Coaching by Cornerstone, where he advises executives, business owners, and young entrepreneurs. When he isn't working his day job (or fishing), Steve writes and speaks often on topics related to strategy, work, and faith. After publishing the *Life@Work* Magazine some years ago, Steve recently launched a new writing and publishing venture, *stephenrgraves.com*. Through this venture, Steve is helping to stage conversations and create content around four life passions: Organizational Strategy, Social Innovation, Leadership Development, and Practical Faith. To learn more, check out his weekly blog and look for the next book coming out soon

Dr. Stephen R. Graves, Executive Coach & Author

Notes

Notes